Keyboarding Quick Reference Guide

Debra J. Housel, M.S.Ed.

ISBN: 0-538-629118

1 2 3 4 5 6 7 8 K 00 99 98 97 96 95 94

Printed in the United States of America

Executive Editor:	Karen Schmohe
Developmental Editor:	Susan Richardson
Marketing Manager:	Larry Qualls
Product Manager:	Al Roane
Production Manager:	Deborah Luebbe

I(T)P
International Thomson Publishing

South-Western Publishing Co. is an ITP Company. The ITP trademark is used under license.

Contents

Introduction to
Keyboarding Quick Reference Guide

Purpose

Keyboarding Quick Reference Guide will demonstrate how to attractively and easily format all types of business documents. Each document type is illustrated with specific formatting directions given within the text of the model documents. In many cases, just a glance at the document models will quickly provide all of the formatting information you need. Also, many formatting tasks (e.g., horizontal and vertical centering) are presented with step-by-step directions.

Focus

In *Keyboarding Quick Reference Guide*, document format receives primary attention because good formatting contributes significantly to the effectiveness of written communications. Format is not simply a matter of appearance. The proper use of format features contributes to the quality of documents by enhancing readability, adding structure, and providing appropriate emphasis. In addition, many of today's sophisticated word processing software packages offer numerous features (such as italic, bold, varied type size and fonts, special characters, boxes, vertical and horizontal lines, and imported graphics) to create a desired effect. *Keyboarding Quick Reference Guide* helps computer users take full advantage of their word processors' capabilities through its sensible page layout tips and illustrations.

Who needs the *Reference Guide?*

Practically all professionals today and in the future will need to understand document formatting, since managers, scientists, engineers, attorneys, physicians, and others have begun to format their own documents while composing them. *Keyboarding Quick Reference Guide* can save its users valuable time. Since much of the information is displayed visually, you can rapidly access what you need and get right back to work. If you are a visual learner, this is the book for you!

Keyboarding Quick Reference Guide addresses every keyboard user's needs by showing how a finished document should look and by giving brief, to-the-point instructions for computer AND typewriter users.

Special Features

The icons (small illustrations of a diskette and a typewriter) that appear at the top of the pages indicate whether the directions apply to computer users, typewriter users, or both.

The "Tips for Word Processors" boxes clue computer users to check their software for time-saving features.

The spiral binding keeps the pages flat so you can key your own document while simultaneously following the *Reference Guide's* directions and seeing what the finished document should look like.

The "Communications Skills Appendix" helps you to determine if your punctuation, number, word division, and other language elements are correct—to ensure that your documents convey a professional tone and can be clearly understood.

Section 1

Formatting Basics

Paper Size and Line Spacing

Margin Setting

Centering

Enumerations

Keying Leaders

Line Ending Bell Use

Justification

Page Layout Enhancements

Paper Length and
Lines Available on Paper

With standard line spacing, each vertical inch on a page contains 6 line spaces. There-fore, to find the number of lines available on any sheet of paper, multiply:

PAPER LENGTH (in inches) X   **6** (lines per inch)   = **TOTAL LINES AVAILABLE**
For example: **8.5**   **x   6**   **= 51**

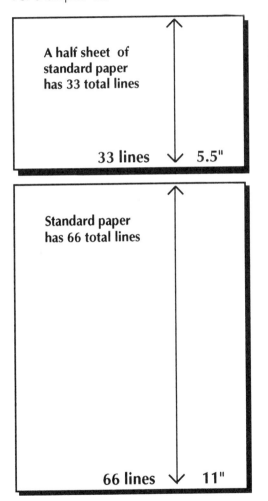

A half sheet of
standard paper
has 33 total lines

33 lines ↓ **5.5"**

Standard paper
has 66 total lines

66 lines ↓ **11"**

Legal paper has
84 total lines

84 lines ↓ **14"**

■ **Tips for Word Processors**
Your word processor may indicate vertical position in inches. If your computer shows you're on line 1.5", just multiply by 6 to find out what line number you're on:

1.5" X 6 = line 9

Paper Width/
Character Spaces Available

The number of characters available across a page depends on the type size or type pitch used.

Typewriters.   10-pitch PICA* type contains 10 characters per inch (cpi)

xxxxxxxxxx

1"

12-pitch ELITE type contains 12 characters per inch

xxxxxxxxxxxx

1"

*Please note that the word PICA applies to a unit of measurement as well as to a typewriter typeface. In desktop publishing, a "pica" is a short unit of space--6 picas are equal to a 1-inch space.

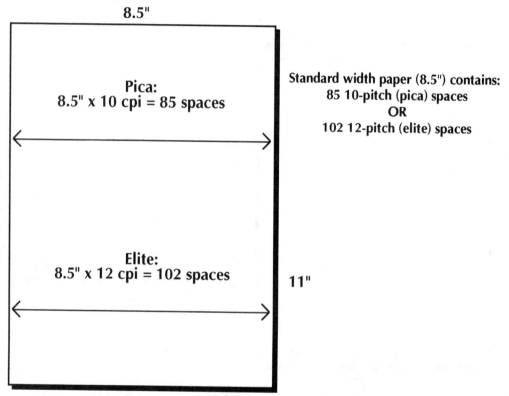

8.5"

Pica:
8.5" x 10 cpi = 85 spaces

Elite:
8.5" x 12 cpi = 102 spaces

11"

Standard width paper (8.5") contains:
85 10-pitch (pica) spaces
OR
102 12-pitch (elite) spaces

Computers.   Multiple typefaces (and sizes) are available with word processing software. Some common default typefaces are the same size and take up the same space as 10- and 12-pitch typewriter fonts:

```
Courier (10 cpi) = 10-pitch or pica type
Prestige elite (12 cpi) = 12-pitch or elite type
```

Line Space Settings

Single Spacing

SINGLE SPACING means typing on every line with 0 blank
lines between each line. These lines are single spaced.

Double Spacing

DOUBLE SPACING means typing on every other line with

1 blank line between each line. These lines are double

spaced.

Quadruple Spacing

QUADRUPLE SPACING means typing on every fourth line

with 3 blank lines between each line. These lines are

quadruple spaced.

Typical Top Margins
for Documents

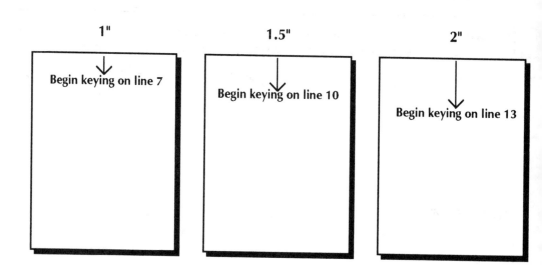

1"

Begin keying on line 7

1.5"

Begin keying on line 10

2"

Begin keying on line 13

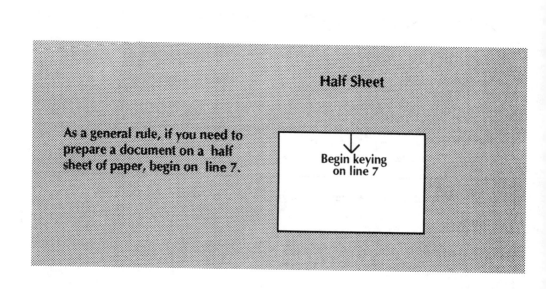

Half Sheet

As a general rule, if you need to prepare a document on a half sheet of paper, begin on line 7.

Begin keying
on line 7

Typical Side Margins for Documents

Shown here are typical margin settings used with 8.5" x 11" paper. Refer to individual document models throughout this guide to determine which margins suit the kind of document you are preparing.

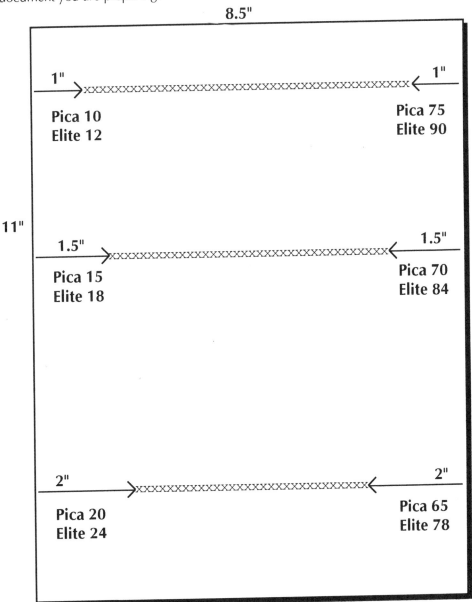

Standard and Customized Elite Margins

Standard Side Margins
Note that the wider the side margins, the narrower the line of type.

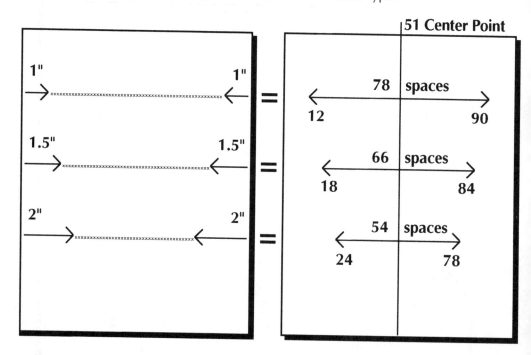

By Inches   **By Spaces in Line**

Customized Side Margins
Suppose you want a 50-space line:
1. Divide 50 by 2. (result is 25)
2. Subtract from center point of 51. (51-25 = **26** Left Margin)
3. Add to 51. (25+51=**76** Right Margin)

Text begins at the left margin position **26** and ends approximately at the right margin position of **76.**

Standard and
Customized Pica Margins

Standard Side Margins

Note that the wider the side margins, the narrower the line of type.

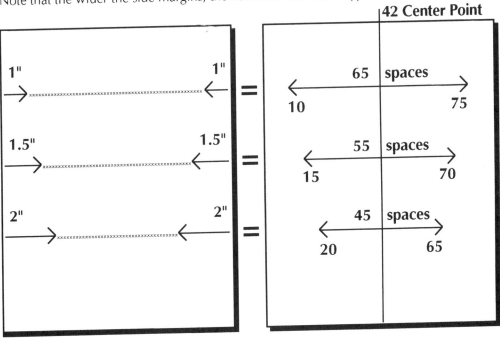

By Inches   **By Spaces in Line**

Customized Side Margins

Suppose you want a 50-space line:

1. Divide 50 by 2. (result is 25)
2. Subtract from center point of 42. (42-25=**17** Left Margin)
3. Add to 42. (42 + 25= 67 **R**ight Margin)

Text begins at the left margin and ends approximately at the right margin.

Vertical Centering
Guide

When information is vertically centered, the space from the top of the paper to the first line of text is the same as the space below the last line of text to the bottom of the paper.

If your word processor does not have a Center Page capability or you work on a typewriter, follow this **HUSH** formula to determine the line on which to begin typing :

How many lines are available on the paper? (33 half sheet paper)
(66 standard paper)
(84 legal paper)
Use   How many lines will the problem use? (Count the text lines and any blank lines needed for double spacing!)

Subtract these two numbers.

Half   Divide the answer in half.
If the number that results is a fraction, disregard the fraction.

+ 1   If an odd number results, add one.

= Space down from top of page this number of lines. Begin keying.

■   **Tips for Word Processors**
There may be a series of commands to make the computer vertically center a document for you. Check your software's instruction manual to see if you have the CENTER PAGE capability.

Vertical
Centering Example

Your supervisor wants you to vertically center this double-spaced announcement on a full sheet of paper.

STAFF NIGHT OUT

Sponsored by the Hurrah Club

Wednesday, October 24, 19--

$8 Advance Tickets are Limited!

Tickets available beginning Friday

COME JOIN US!

How many lines are available	66
Use how many	-11
Subtract them	55
Half that number	27½ (drop the ½)
Add one	+1
Start keying on line	28

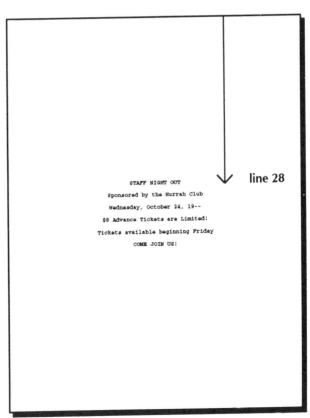

Horizontal Centering—Computers

The heading of this page is horizontally centered. The middle of the heading is positioned at the exact horizontal center point of the paper.

1. Most word processing software centers text between the side margins. Therefore, you must set your left and right margins before you use the centering feature.

2. Press the centering command keys. Depending on your machine, this may be a function key , or CONTROL + another key , or ALT + another key.

3. Key the text.

4. If you make a keying error, backspace and correct the error. This will not turn off the centering function.

5. Press the ENTER key. The program will automatically back up and center the item between the left and right margins.

6. The centering function automatically turns off.

■ **Tips for Word Processors**

If you have several consecutive lines of type to center horizontally, see if your software offers CENTER JUSTIFICATION. Simply activate this feature, key the lines to be centered, then turn off CENTER JUSTIFICATION. This feature is especially useful for announcements and invitations.

Horizontal
Centering—Typewriters

The heading of this page is horizontally centered. The center point of the heading is positioned at the exact horizontal center of the page.

1. Begin at the centerpoint of the page. (**51** elite, **42** pica)

2. Backspace once for every 2 characters and spaces.

3. If necessary, IGNORE a leftover character--to center the example below you would backspace 11 spaces from the center point.

4. Key in the text.

```
       1  2  3  4   5  6   7  8   9 10 11
       Ma/te/ri/al/ T/o /Be/ C/en/te/re/d
        <  <  <  <  <  <   <   <  <  <  <
```

Enumerations—Indented Format

Enumerations are lists of numbered or lettered sentences. Use the indented format with documents containing indented paragraphs or when the enumerations in a block format document require special emphasis.

1. Single space the enumerated items and double space between the items.
2. Key the number, period (followed by 2 spaces), and the rest of the first line.
3. Indent the second and succeeding lines of each enumeration four spaces or to your first tab position (depending on your software). This way, all lines block at the same point, with only the number or letter remaining at the left margin.
4. If your document contains paragraphs that are indented, you must indent the entire enumeration ½" (5 spaces) from the left margin of the main document. (For example, if the letter's left margin is 1" or 10 spaces in, the enumeration begins at 1 ½" or 15 spaces in.) Proceed to indent the second and succeeding lines by using your tab key.

With Indented Paragraphs

Dear Ms. Mastrodonato

Tab ➞ As you requested, I have enclosed a copy of the Edison-Phillips Central School District's Continuing Education Catalog for Fall 19--. You will find information regarding the Anyone Can Swim Program on page 15. When you register your child remember to

  1. Fill out a parent/guardian's name and address in the space provided at the top of the registration form.

  2. Put the child's name and age on the line directly under the session number for which you are registering.

With Block Paragraphs

Dear Ms. Mastrodonato

As you requested, I have enclosed a copy of the Edison-Phillips Central School District's Continuing Education Catalog for Fall 19--. You will find information regarding the Anyone Can Swim Program on page 15. When you register your child remember to

1. Fill out a parent/guardian's name and address in the spaces provided at the top of the registration form.

2. Put the child's name and age on the line directly under the session number for which you are registering.

■ **Tips for Word Processors**
Use the left-margin-only indent feature, if available.

Enumerations—Block Format

Enumerations are lists of numbered or lettered sentences. Use the block format for enumerations in documents formatted with blocked paragraphs (not indented paragraphs).

1. Single space the enumerated items and double space between the items.

2. Key the number at the left margin, following the period with two spaces.

3. Key second and succeeding lines also at the left margin. On a computer, word wrap will correctly position the second and succeeding lines.

```
Dear Ms. Mastrodonato

As you requested, I have enclosed a copy of the Edison-
Phillips Central School District's Continuing Education
Catalog for Fall 19--.  You will find information regarding
the Anyone Can Swim Program on page 15.  When you register
your child, remember to

1.  Fill out a parent/guardian's name and address in the
spaces provided at the top of the registration form.

2.  Put the child's name and age on the line directly under
the session number for which you are registering.

3.  Be certain you select the class with the date, time, and
session number that correspond to your child's age group.
```

Leaders

Leaders guide a reader's eyes to information presented in columns. They are made by alternating spaces with periods. On many computers, you can set a "leader tab" for the column where you want the leaders to end. Consult your software's documentation to use this feature.

If your program does not have leader tabs, follow these steps:

1. Key the first item in the first column.

2. Space ONCE and then press the period key. Note whether the period is on an ODD or an EVEN space.

3. Continue to press the space bar and period key, alternating across the page.

4. Stop the leaders approximately 3 spaces before the beginning of the second column.

5. Be sure to key all leaders on odd or even spaces, according to what you determined in Step 2.

```
        grams . . . . . . . . . . . . .   gms
        milligrams . . . . . . . . . .    mgs
        pound . . . . . . . . . . . . .   lb
        ounces  . . . . . . . . . . . .   oz
        tablespoon . . . . . . . . . .    tbsp
        teaspoon . . . . . . . . . . .    tsp
```

Note that leaders never touch either the first or second column. The leaders above are keyed on every even space; this aligns them so that you could draw a straight vertical line through them.

To see another example of leaders, refer to the Table of Contents model on page 50.

Line Ending Bell Use

To decide how to end a line, follow these rules:

1. A typewriter's bell rings approximately 6-10 spaces BEFORE its right margin stop so you can decide where to end that line.

2. Finish the word you are keying when the bell rings.

3. If the next word is short (2 or 3 characters), key it on that line.

4. If the next word has more than 3 characters, you will usually key it on the next line.

5. If the next word has 6 or more characters, you may be able to divide it following the word division rules listed in this reference guide.

6. Divide as few words as possible. NEVER end 3 or more consecutive lines with divided words.

7. Never stop keying more than 3 spaces before the margin stop.

8. Never divide the last word on a page.

Refer to Line Break Rules on page 97 for more specific guidelines for breaking lines and refer to Word Division Rules on pages 98-99 for specific guidelines for dividing words at the ends of lines.

Justification

There are four types of justification that most software programs can produce:

Right justification.   Used when you want text to align at the right margin, leaving the left margin ragged (uneven). This is an example of right justification:

```
                           Patient:   Joe Henson
                            Doctor:   E. J. Schwartz
                   Date of Visit:   November 29, 19--
```

Left justification.   Used when you want text to align at the left margin, leaving a ragged (uneven) right margin. Some people feel this makes the document look like it was personally keyed as opposed to "processed" on a computer. This is an example of left justification:

```
I am writing to request that you send a letter of recom-
mendation on my behalf for the position of administra-
tive assistant to Mr. Tyrone Henry, vice president of
Allied Computer Services.  I have already been called to
come in for an interview once the holidays are over.
```

Center justification.   Used when you have several lines in a row which you wish to center. This is faster than centering each line individually. This is an example of center justification:

```
           Mr. and Mrs. Harvey Woods
            are pleased to announce
         the engagement of their daughter
               Marlene Rochelle
```

Full justification.   Used when you want identical (even) right and left margins. Extra internal spaces are added in each line of text wherever necessary to create this effect. This is an example of full justification:

```
I  am  writing  to  request  that  you  send  a  letter  of
recommendation on my behalf for the position of administra-
tive assistant to Mr. Tyrone Henry, vice president of Allied
Computer Services.  I have already been called to come in
for an interview once the holidays are over.
```

Page Layout Enhancements for Typewriters

When using a typewriter to format a document, four features can add structure, increase readability, and provide emphasis:

- Spacing
- <u>Underlining</u>
- CAPITAL LETTERS
- **Bold** (on electronic typewriters only)

1. To show the importance of a title, key it in solid capitals and leave extra space below it to set it off from the body of the document.

2. Use indenting to add structure to the document. Be consistent by indenting all information of the same type or similar importance within the same document.

3. Employ numbers or alphabetical characters to set off the items in an enumeration (list).

4. Underline and use extra space above and below information that should be set apart from the main body of the text (for example, side headings in a report).

5. If available, utilize bold on the title or in place of underlining. Be sure to use the bold feature sparingly, or it will lose its effect.

6. Beware of using too many features on one item! For example, it would be overkill to bold, underline, and set apart with extra line spaces a side heading.

Page Layout Enhancements
for Computers

When using a computer to format a document, many word processsing features add structure, increase readability, and provide emphasis:

- Spacing
- <u>Underlining</u>
- CAPITAL LETTERS
- **Bold**
- Use of different type sizes

- Use of different typestyles
- *Italics*
- Imported graphics
- Use of bullets with enumerated items
- Use of full justification

To see these features "in action" refer to the Letters in Transition, Reports in Transition, and Tables in Transition models on pages 39, 59, and 75.

1. To emphasize the importance of a title, use all caps, bold it, or use a larger font of the same or different typestyle as the rest of the document. DO NOT go overboard by using more than two of these features at once. You can also leave extra space below the title to set it off from the body of the document.

2. Utilize left-side only indent (hanging) to add structure to the document. Be consistent by indenting all information of the same type or of similar importance within the same document.

3. Employ bullets, numbers, or alphabetical characters to set off the items in an enumeration (list).

4. Underline and use extra space above and below internal information that should be set apart from the main body of the text (for example, side headings in a report). You can also utilize bold in place of the underlining. However, use the bold feature sparingly, or it will lose its effect.

5. Use serif typestyles for lengthy text because they help to guide the eye across a line of type. (Serif type has short extension angled at the "tails" of letter. This sentence is typeset with serif type.) Use sans serif type with small amounts of text (for example, when a graphic is accompanied by a brief explanation). Sans serif type does not have the serif extensions. **This sentence is typeset with sans serif type.**

6. *Use italic type (like this sentence) only to emphasize important information or to set aside an internal heading.* Titles of published works are usually set in italics.

7. Full justification (even right and left margins) gives a document a professional, published appearance.

REMEMBER: Check your printer's capabilities! Even if your software has the capacity to produce some of these features, your printer may not.

Correspondence

Letter Placement Guides

Letter Formats

Memorandum Formats

Second-Page Headings

Envelopes

Letters in Transition

Letter Placement Guide

The information below will help you attractively position block and modified block letters of short, average, or long lengths. (Refer to the models on pages 30 and 31 for Simplified and Personal-Business Letters.) Note that standard placement is easy to remember and is efficient, while variable placement is generally more attractive.

Special notations in a letter (for example, a subject line, enclosure notation, copy notation, or postscript) require raising the dateline 1 line for every 2 such features.

Letter Length	Variable Side Margins	Standard Side Margins	Variable Dateline Placement	Standard Dateline Placement
Under 100 words (short)	2"	1"	line 18 (2.83")	line 13 (2")
101-200 words (average)	1.5"	1"	line 16 (2.67")	line 13 (2")
Over 201 words (long)	1"	1"	line 14 (2.3")	line 13 (2")

Note: When using a letterhead, be sure that the dateline is always at least a double space below the letterhead.

Elite/Pica Side Margins

	Elite	Pica
2"	24-78	20-65
1.5"	18-84	15-70
1"	12-90	10-75

Short Letter—Standard and Variable Placement

Jones Mfg Inc
5555 W. Fifth St.
New York, NY 10101

May 13, 19--   **2" OR line 13** ↓

Ms. Annette T. Morningstar
Business Department Chair
Rush-Wheatland High School
Grand Forks, ND 58210-1789

1"

1"

Dear Ms. Morningstar:

I am delighted that four of your accounting education students have
chosen to do their internship at our company starting June 10.

I plan to meet with Dawn
Milagros Vargas, and Zac
students report to the H
B on Charity Boulevard.
to them then.

Again, we look forward t
with our organization.

Very sincerely yours,

Edward John Hill
Human Resources Director

rt

Jones Mfg Inc
5555 W. Fifth St.
New York, NY 10101

May 13, 19--   **2.83" OR line 18** ↓

Ms. Annette T. Morningstar
Business Department Chair
Rush-Wheatland High School
Grand Forks, ND 58210-1789

Dear Ms. Morningstar:

I am delighted that four of your accounting
education students have chosen to do their
internship at our company starting June 10.

I plan to meet with Dawn Beasom, Sarah Lynn
Gastman, Cindy Jackson, Milagros Vargas, and
Zachary White on June 10. Please have these
students report to the Human Resources Office,
located in Building B on Charity Boulevard.
Their work assignments will be explained to
them then.

Again, we look forward to having your students
do their internship with our organization.

Very sincerely yours,

Edward John Hill
Human Resources Director

rt

2"

2"

Standard Placement

- Top margin: 2"
  (line 13)
- Side margins: 1"
  elite   12   90
  pica   10   75

Variable Placement

- Top margin: 2.83"
  (line 18)
- Side margins: 2"
  elite   24   78
  pica   20   65

24

Average Letter

Variable Placement

- Top margin: 2.67"
  (line 16)
- Side margins: 1.5"
  elite 18 84
  pica 15 70

Super Z-TEK *Electronics*
125 Ashley Road
Peach Valley, NH 03301-3158

June 25, 19--   2.67" OR line 16 ⌄

Mr. Walter Malthaner
Gordon-Walker Electronics, Inc.
2438 Castle Road
Edgewater, FL 33552-4954

Dear Mr. Malthaner

1.5"   Thank you for your letter requesting information on our   1.5"
new Z-10 microprocessor. Several vendors of software
development tools h
corporation and the

Enclosed is our mar
complete specificat
high-speed peripher
our phone conversat
some application no
cost product.

I have asked our sa
Lee, to contact you
components. Please
more material. Tha
products.

Yours truly

Roxanne Dunn
Sales Manager

cr

Super Z-TEK *Electronics*
125 Ashley Road
Peach Valley, NH 03301-3158

June 25, 19--   2" OR line 13 ⌄

Mr. Walter Malthaner
Gordon-Walker Electronics, Inc.
2438 Castle Road
Edgewater, FL 33552-4954

Dear Mr. Malthaner

1"   Thank you for your letter requesting information on our new Z-10   1"
microprocessor. Several vendors of software development tools
have recently signed on with our corporation and the Z-10.

Enclosed is our marketing release packet containing complete
specifications for the Z-10 and our line of high-speed peripheral
chips that support it. Based on our phone conversation of June 4,
I have also included some application notes on how to use our chips
in a low-cost product.

I have asked our sales representative for your area, Jan Lee, to
contact you to assist you in evaluating our components. Please
contact me again if you would like more material. Thank you
again for considering our products.

Yours truly

Roxanne Dunn
Sales Manager

cr

Standard Placement

- Top margin: 2"
  (line 13)
- Side margins: 1"
  elite 12 90
  pica 10 75

Long Letter

GORDO-WALKER ELECTRONICS
3284 HOLLYBROOK ROAD
EDGEWATER, FL 33552-4954
(407) 336-2399

July 1, 19--   ▼   **2.3" OR line 14**

Ms. Anne Marie Rossner
Marketing Specialist
Super Z-TEK Electronics Corporation
125 Ashley Road
Peach Valley, NH 03301-3158

Dear Ms. Rossner

1"   I appreciated the information you sent me about your new Z-10   1"
microprocessor. Your prompt response to my request coupled with
the expert help of your local sales representative, Jan Lee, helped
to me convince my management to take a closer look at your line of
products.

Your products really sta
have been working with W
they have not yet releas
Alpha40 microprocessor.
organization have actual
phone. In contrast, Ms.
the "extra mile" to ensu
make an informed decisio

Since Ms. Lee is current
two sets of the new manu
We are eager to begin pl
sor with our latest inno

Sincerely

Walter Malthaner
Quality Control Coordina

ws

Variable Placement

- **Top margin: 2.3"**
  (line 14)
- **Side margins: 1"**
  elite   12   90
  pica   10   75

GORDO-WALKER ELECTRONICS
3284 HOLLYBROOK ROAD
EDGEWATER, FL 33552-4954
(407) 336-2399

July 1, 19--   ▼   **2" OR line 13**

Ms. Anne Marie Rossner
Marketing Specialist
Super Z-TEK Electronics Corporation
125 Ashley Road
Peach Valley, NH 03301-3158

Dear Ms. Rossner

1"   I appreciated the information you sent me about your new Z-10   1"
microprocessor. Your prompt response to my request coupled with
the expert help of your local sales representative, Jan Lee, helped
to me convince my management to take a closer look at your line of
products.

Your products really stack up well against your competitors. We
have been working with Wyatt Technology for three months now, and
they have not yet released the final specifications for their
Alpha40 microprocessor. In addition, members of their marketing
organization have actually been rude to some of my coworkers on the
phone. In contrast, Ms. Lee has cheerfully and efficiently gone
the "extra mile" to ensure that we had all the data necessary to
make an informed decision.

Since Ms. Lee is currently on vacation, would you please send me
two sets of the new manuals for the compiler as soon as possible.
We are eager to begin planning the integration of your microprocessor with our latest innovation. Thank you for all of your help.

Sincerely

Walter Malthaner
Quality Control Coordinator

ws

Standard Placement

- **Top margin: 2"**
  (line 13)
- **Side margins: 1"**
  elite   12   90
  pica   10   75

Letter Parts

July 13, 19-- **Date**

Dr. Jesus Nieves **Inside address**
Hannan Community College
5674 Skytop Drive
Blair, NE 68008-5674

Dear Dr. Nieves **Salutation**

EMPLOYMENT OPPORTUNITIES **Subject line**

Would recent graduates from your office technology/administration
program enjoy the variety of assignments that the ProWorker Temporary
Agency offers? We provide temporary office help to a wide variety of
organizations in assignments ranging from a few days to an entire year.
As a result, our associates can gain desirable experience in many types
of firms.

Since quite a few of our employees take permanent positions with the
firms to which they were assigned, we must continuously recruit new
workers. The enclosed job descriptions outline the general duties and
qualifications of the employees we need. Note that we are especially
in need of word processors with integrated spreadsheet and data base
knowledge.

If any of your graduates would be interested in temporary employment,
please have them contact my administrative assistant, Edward Dole, at
189-4047 to arrange for interviews.

Sincerely yours **Complimentary close**

PROWORKERS TEMPORARY AGENCY **Company name**

Mrs. Desiree L. Sayles **Writer's name**
Personnel Manager **Writer's title**

db **Reference initials**

Enclosures (5) **Enclosure notation**

c Edward Dole **Copy notation**

Postscript

For your information, we've hired over fifty Hannan Community College
graduates over the last two years.

■ **Tips for Word Processors**

The words within the complimentary close, writer and writer's title, and
reference initials are good places to utilize **macros**--series of keystrokes
stored under particular names that appear on the screen when activated.
Macros usually consist of frequently used formats, terms and phrases, and
commands. By spending a little time creating macros, you can save a lot of
time throughout your workday. Refer to your specific software's instruction
manual.

Block Letter

WORKPLACE

DESIGN

ASSOCIATES

1955 Water Road
Halley, CA 20001-9861

February 14, 19-- **4 (QS)**

Mr. Thurman Johnson
Sunscape Construction
1475 Brantwood Drive
Buffalo, NY 14412-5134   **2 (DS)**

Dear Mr. Johnson   **2**

This letter is prepared in block format. This format is efficient because EVERYTHING blocks at the left margin. In addition,
it is a very easy format for office personnel to learn how to
prepare, and it looks businesslike.

Use standard or variable letter placement with this format.
(Standard placement is shown). No punctuation follows the
salutation and complimentary close. This is called open punctuation and is used because it saves keystrokes. The person who
prepares the letter keys his reference initials a double space
below the closing lines. If there is an enclosure for the
letter, the word Enclosure is keyed a double space below the
reference initials. Copy notations are placed a double space
below the enclosure notation (as shown below).

I am pleased to enclose our booklet entitled Letter Styles for
the 1990s. Please contact me if you have any further questions. **2**

Sincerely yours   **4**

Ms. Katrina E. McAllister
Document Specialist   **2**

xx **2**

Enclosure **2**

c Huang Ko Fung

Modified Block Letter

Business Consulting Services
726 Westcott Boulevard
Baltimore, MD 62103-8726

Position date at center point
September 18, 19--
4 (QS)

Dr. Karen Nolanski
New Design Educational Enterprises
1713 Wildwood Acres
Columbus, OH 42150-1332
2 (DS)

Dear Dr. Nolanski:
2

    This letter is prepared in modified block format.
This format is very popular and has been in use for a
long time. It is an easy format for office personnel
to learn to prepare, and it is attractive. The date and
complimentary closing lines are keyed at the center
point of the page. This is the only letter style in
which you may choose to indent the paragraphs (fivespace
tab).

    Use standard or variable letter placement (vari-
able is shown). You may note that punctuation follows
the salutation and complimentary close. This is called
mixed punctuation and is frequently used in business
letters. The person who prepares the letter keys his
reference initials a double space below the closing
lines. If there is an enclosure for the letter, the
word Enclosure is keyed a double space below the
reference initials. Copy notations are placed a double
space below the enclosure notation.

    I am pleased to enclose our booklet entitled
Correspondence in the 1990s. Please contact me if you
have any further questions.
2

                 Sincerely yours,
4

                 Mrs. Mariangela Annucci
                 Document Specialist
2

eb
2
                 **Position closing lines and writer's
name at center point**

Enclosure
2

c Helen Rigard

29

Simplified Letter

Electronic Mail Corporation

1578 Miramar Road

Philadelphia, PA 26310-1578

January 27, 19--
4 (QS)
1.83" (line 12) with window envelope
2.17" (line 14) with regular envelope

MS TANYSHA BAXTER
HAWTHORNE DOYLE & SPRATT ESQ
6221 NORTH ROSE AVENUE
LOS ANGELES CA 90058-6221
2 (DS)

SIMPLIFIED BLOCK LETTER FORMAT
2

This document illustrates the Simplified Block Letter. Its
many practical, time-saving features are making it popular.

1. The date is placed on line 12 so that the address will
show through the window of a window envelope. The date may be
placed on line 4 when a regular envelope is used.

2. The address is keyed in all-cap letters, with no punctuation, as recommended by the United States Postal Service for
faster processing. The address may be keyed in cap/lowercase
letters when regular envelopes are used.

3. An all-capitals subject line replaces the traditional
salutation to aid in speedy document filing and location.

4. The complimentary close is omitted.

5. One-inch standard margins are used for all simplified
letters, regardless of their length.

All of these features are designed to bring greater efficiency
to the electronic processing of mail.
4

JUAN T. FERNANDEZ, DIRECTOR

dh

1"
elite 12
pica 10

1"
elite 90
pica 75

Personal-Business Letter

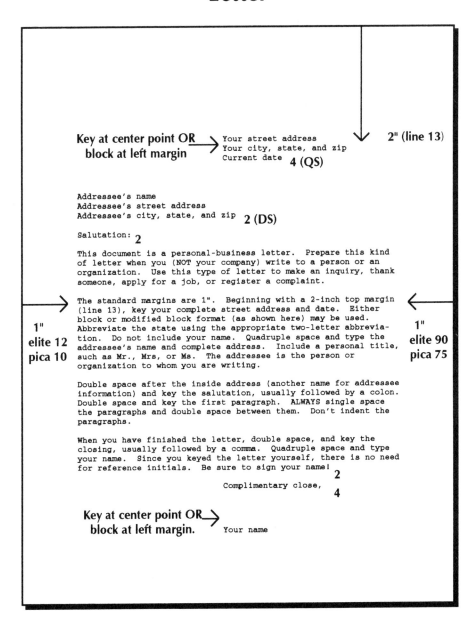

Key at center point OR → Your street address   ↓   2" (line 13)
block at left margin   Your city, state, and zip
                                  Current date **4 (QS)**

Addressee's name
Addressee's street address
Addressee's city, state, and zip **2 (DS)**

Salutation: **2**

This document is a personal-business letter. Prepare this kind
of letter when you (NOT your company) write to a person or an
organization. Use this type of letter to make an inquiry, thank
someone, apply for a job, or register a complaint.

1"
elite 12
pica 10

The standard margins are 1". Beginning with a 2-inch top margin
(line 13), key your complete street address and date. Either
block or modified block format (as shown here) may be used.
Abbreviate the state using the appropriate two-letter abbreviation. Do not include your name. Quadruple space and type the
addressee's name and complete address. Include a personal title,
such as Mr., Mrs, or Ms. The addressee is the person or
organization to whom you are writing.

1"
elite 90
pica 75

Double space after the inside address (another name for addressee
information) and key the salutation, usually followed by a colon.
Double space and key the first paragraph. ALWAYS single space
the paragraphs and double space between them. Don't indent the
paragraphs.

When you have finished the letter, double space, and key the
closing, usually followed by a comma. Quadruple space and type
your name. Since you keyed the letter yourself, there is no need
for reference initials. Be sure to sign your name! **2**

                      Complimentary close, **4**

Key at center point OR →
block at left margin.   Your name

31

Special Features in Letters

Taylor, Ling, and Blackhawk 1070 Warf Street Milwaukee, WI 53202-7001

June 22, 19--

2(DS)

REGISTERED 2 **Mailing Notation**

Attention Ms. Edelia Ortiz **Attention Line**
Compu-Tron, Inc.
5687 Jefferson Road
Buffalo, NY 14426-9204 2

Dear Administrative Assistant: 2

Subject: Special Features in Business Letters 2 **Subject Line**

This letter shows the appropriate format for special features
on business letters. REGISTERED is a mailing notation; so are
CERTIFIED, INSURED, CONFIDENTIAL, AIRMAIL, and SPECIAL DELIVERY.

When an attention line is used, the salutation does not refer
to the mentioned person (in this case, Ms. Ortiz). An attention
line is used when you want the letter to be opened in the event of the
addressee's absence. Block the subject line when the paragraphs are
blocked; indent it when paragraphs are indented.

If you include several enclosures, put the number of enclosures in
parentheses after the word "Enclosures". The copy notation (c) is
followed by the name of the person to whom the copy is going; it NEVER
indicates the file copy. When used, the postscript is always the last
line in the letter. If the letter has indented paragraphs, you
may also indent the postscript notation.

When you have several special features within a letter, raise the
dateline one line for every two special features. The dateline must
remain at least a double space below the letterhead.

2

Sincerely yours,

2

Company name TAYLOR, LING, AND BLACKHAWK 4 (QS)

Edric J. Chang
Correspondence Specialist 2

db 2

Enclosure(S) 2 2 **Enclosure notation**

c Enrico Lopez 2

Only the attention line and the mailing notations go on the envelope. **Postscript**
Refer to the page entitled Addressing Envelopes.

Standard Memorandum Format

An interoffice memorandum (memo) is used for communication WITHIN an organization. It is not mailed through the U.S. Postal Service. Many organizations using computers no longer use preprinted forms. If your organization does not use preprinted memorandum forms, use plain paper or blank letterhead paper and make your own guide words (To:, From:, Date:, Subject:)as shown in the example below.

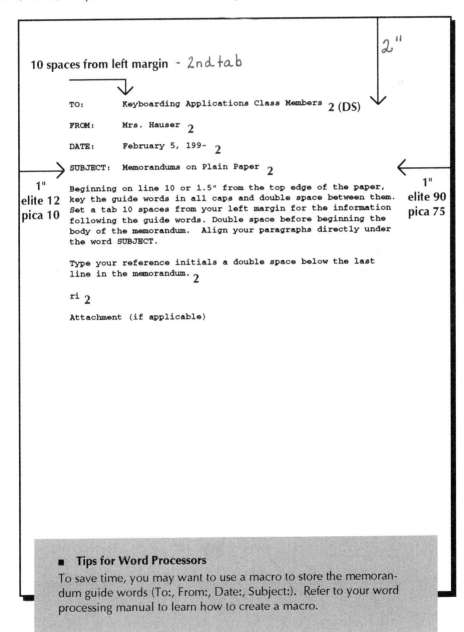

10 spaces from left margin - 2nd tab

2"

TO: Keyboarding Applications Class Members 2 (DS)

FROM: Mrs. Hauser 2

DATE: February 5, 199- 2

SUBJECT: Memorandums on Plain Paper 2

1"
elite 12
pica 10

Beginning on line 10 or 1.5" from the top edge of the paper,
key the guide words in all caps and double space between them.
Set a tab 10 spaces from your left margin for the information
following the guide words. Double space before beginning the
body of the memorandum. Align your paragraphs directly under
the word SUBJECT.

1"
elite 90
pica 75

Type your reference initials a double space below the last
line in the memorandum. 2

ri 2

Attachment (if applicable)

■ **Tips for Word Processors**
To save time, you may want to use a macro to store the memorandum guide words (To:, From:, Date:, Subject:). Refer to your word processing manual to learn how to create a macro.

Memorandum/Preprinted Form

Interoffice memorandums (memos) are used for communication WITHIN an organization and are not mailed through the U.S. Postal Service. If your organization uses computers and preprinted forms, you may prepare memos with an electronic template. The directions below apply to typewriter users using preprinted memorandum forms.

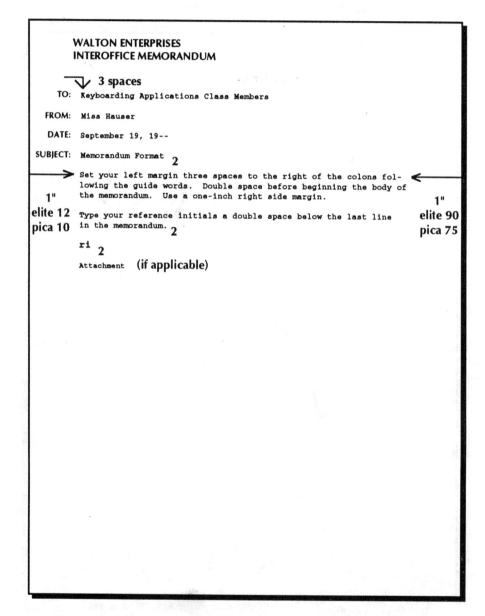

Simplified
Memorandum

October 19, 19-- 4 (QS)   ↓ 1.5" (line 10) OR 2" (line 13)

Office Staff 2 (DS)

SIMPLIFIED MEMORANDUM FORMAT 2

Effective at the first of the month, we are utilizing the simplified memorandum format for all internal correspondence. This memo
is a visual example of this type of document. 2

1"
elite 12
pica 10

Use a 1.5" or 2" top margin and 1" side margins. Key the date,
return 4 times, and key the addressee's name. Double space and
put the subject line in all caps or cap/lowercase. Then double
space and key the body single spaced, double spacing only between
paragraphs. After you have completed the body, quadruple space
and key the author's name and title. Don't forget to include your
reference initials.

1"
elite 90
pica 75

Using this format should make our internal correspondence easier
to prepare, read, and file. If you have any questions, please
consult your immediate supervisor. 4

Milagros Sanchez, Vice President for Communications
hb

Second Page
Heading (Letter or Memo)

Addressee's Name   ↓   1" (line 7)
Page 2
Date
   2 (DS)

This is an example of the heading for the second page of a letter
or memorandum. Whenever these documents go beyond one page, all
additional pages should be headed this way. Second and subsequent
pages are typed on plain paper, not letterhead. Use the same
margins as those on the first page of the document.

         2

If an attention line is used, the first two lines of the letter
address appear in the heading shown above.

Addressing Envelopes

REMEMBER: Use all caps
Omit punctuation

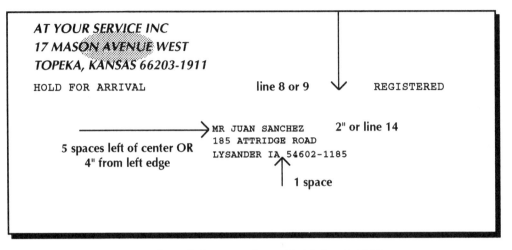

AT YOUR SERVICE INC
17 MASON AVENUE WEST
TOPEKA, KANSAS 66203-1911

HOLD FOR ARRIVAL   line 8 or 9 ↓   REGISTERED

                                  → MR JUAN SANCHEZ   2" or line 14
                                   185 ATTRIDGE ROAD
5 spaces left of center OR LYSANDER IA 54602-1185
4" from left edge

                                     ↑ 1 space

Large/Legal size envelope (9 1/2" x 4 1/8")

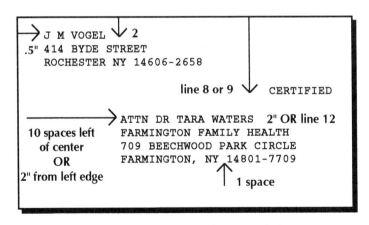

→ J M VOGEL ↓ 2
.5" 414 BYDE STREET
    ROCHESTER NY 14606-2658

                     line 8 or 9 ↓ CERTIFIED

                    → ATTN DR TARA WATERS 2" OR line 12
10 spaces left   FARMINGTON FAMILY HEALTH
of center   709 BEECHWOOD PARK CIRCLE
OR   FARMINGTON, NY 14801-7709
2" from left edge   ↑ 1 space

Small envelope (6 1/2" x 3 5/8")

State Abbreviations
for Use in Addresses

Do not use these abbreviations within the body of a document (letter, memo, report, etc).

Alabama	AL	Montana	MT
Alaska	AK	Nebraska	NE
Arizona	AZ	Nevada	NV
Arkansas	AR	New Hampshire	NH
California	CA	New Jersey	NJ
Colorado	CO	New Mexico	NM
Connecticut	CT	New York	NY
Delaware	DE	North Carolina	NC
District of Columbia	DC	North Dakota	ND
Florida	FL	Ohio	OH
Georgia	GA	Oklahoma	OK
Guam	GU	Oregon	OR
Hawaii	HI	Pennsylvania	PA
Idaho	ID	Puerto Rico	PR
Illinois	IL	Rhode Island	RI
Indiana	IN	South Carolina	SC
Iowa	IA	South Dakota	SD
Kansas	KS	Tennessee	TN
Kentucky	KY	Texas	TX
Louisiana	LA	Utah	UT
Maine	ME	Vermont	VT
Maryland	MD	Virgin Islands	VI
Massachusetts	MA	Virginia	VA
Michigan	MI	Washington	WA
Minnesota	MN	West Virginia	WV
Mississippi	MS	Wisconsin	WI
Missouri	MO	Wyoming	WY

Letters in Transition

Geraldine R. Zukowski
3040 Cottonwood Lane
Blue Skies, WY 69326-3040

December 15, 19--

Ms. Pier Aragau
1308 West Cornwall Drive
Blue Skies, WY 69326-1308

Dear Ms. Aragau

Would you please send a recommendation letter for me for the position of administrative assistant to the vice president of State-of-the-Art Electronics Corporation, Mr. Marcus Henry. I have an interview scheduled with him after the holidays.

This particular administrative assistant position is a fantastic professional opportunity for me because it is so challenging. Since Mr. Henry is frequently out of the office, I would be in charge of keeping the office operating in an efficient manner. Not only would I be expected to have exceptional computer skills, but I would also have to handle clients and make business decisions in Mr. Henry's absence.

Because you are well aware of my capabilities, I would be most grateful if you would send the recommendation letter to the following address: *Mr. Marcus Henry, State-of-the-Art Electronics Corporation, 6459 Apollo Boulevard, Plainfield, Wyoming 69328-6459.* If you are unable to do this for me or if you would like additional information, please call me any evening at 841-0987. Thank you for your assistance, Ms. Aragau. Happy Holidays!

Yours very truly

Geraldine R. Zukowski

Some of the features shown above (bold, italics, full justification) are available on many electronic typewriters as well as most software packages.

Use these features wisely to emphasize essential data or to make important information easy to locate (such as the address to which to send the recommendation letter in the example document).

Section 3

Reports

Report Formats

Additional Report Components

Documentation

Reports in Transition

Unbound Report
(Page 1)

STANDARD FORMAT FOR AN UNBOUND REPORT ↓ **2" (line 13)**

4 (QS)   **OR 1.5" (line 10)**

    Illustrated here is an unbound report. Unbound reports are stapled at the upper left corner, not bound within a folder or binder. Begin by centering the title in all caps 1.5" (line 10) or 2" (line 13) from the top edge of paper. It is no longer necessary for reports prepared in elite type to start on line 12. Users of smaller fonts may prefer the 2" (line 13) option. Quadruple space after the title. If you have a subtitle, key it a double space below the main title and then quadruple space after the subtitle. Double space the report body. Indent paragraphs 5 spaces and use 1" side margins.

1"
elite 12
pica 10

1"
elite 12
pica 10

2 (DS)

    Long quotes of 4 or more lines are single spaced and
indented 5 spaces from the left margin. No quotation ↓ **1 (SS)**
marks are used. Enumerations within a report are formatted in the same way.

2

    Leave a bottom margin of between 1" (6 lines) and 1.5" (9 lines) on each page. Do not number the first page of a report; begin numbering on the second page. Key the page number on line 7 at the right margin point (flush right). Double space and continue with the body.

    You cannot divide the last word on a page. When dividing a paragraph, you must leave at least 2 lines of a paragraph on the first page and carry at least 2 lines of type to the second page. (Remember, these are lines of type, NOT sentences!) The second line carried to a new page may be a partial line.

↑ **1"-1.5" (6-9 blank lines)**

Unbound Report
(Page 2)

1" (line 7)　2 2 (DS)

<u>Side Headings</u> 2

1"　　Side headings are blocked at the left margin and underscored.　　1"
Double space before and after a side heading (such as the one
above this paragraph). 2

　　<u>Paragraph headings</u>. For this type of heading indent 5
spaces, underscore the heading, and use capital and lower case
letters.　 A paragraph heading is actually part of the paragraph
and must be followed by a period.　 This paragraph begins with a
paragraph heading.

■ **Tips for Word Processors:**
Turn on widow and orphan protection to make the word processing
program operate within the page break guidelines explained on the
first page of the Unbound Report model (page 43).

Leftbound Report
(Page 1)

STANDARD FORMAT FOR A LEFTBOUND REPORT   **2" (line 13)**

4 (QS)   **OR 1.5" (line 10)**

1.5"
elite 18
pica 15

Illustrated here is a leftbound report. A leftbound report has a wider left margin than an unbound report to allow for binding in a folder or binder. Begin by centering the title in all caps 1.5" (line 10) or 2" (line 13) from the top edge of the paper. It is no longer necessary for reports prepared in elite type to start on line 12. Users of smaller fonts may prefer the 2" (line 13) option. Backspace center the title from 54 (elite) or 45 (pica). The center point of the paper is "moved" over 3 spaces because the report binder takes up 5 to 6 spaces. If you use the centering feature on your computer, it will automatically adjust the center point for you.

1.5"
elite 18
pica 15

Quadruple space after the title and then begin the body of a report. (If you have a subtitle, position it a double space after the main title and quadruple space after the subtitle.) Use a 1.5" left margin and a 1" right margin and indent paragraphs 5 spaces. Double space the report body.

2

Long quotes of 4 or more lines are single spaced and indented 5 spaces from the left margin. Enumerations within a report are formatted in the same way. 2

Leave a bottom margin of between 1" (6 lines) and 1.5" (9 lines). Do not number the first page of a report; begin numbering on the second page. Type the page number on line 7 at the right margin point (flush right). Double space and continue with the body.

1"-1.5"
(6-9 blank lines)

Leftbound Report
(Page 2)

> Never divide the last word on a page. When dividing the
> last paragraph, you must leave at least 2 lines of the
> paragraph on the first page and carry at least 2 lines of
> type to the second page. (Remember, these are lines of type,
> NOT sentences!) The second line carried to a new page may be
> 1.5"   a partial line. 2   1"
>
> <u>Side Headings</u> 2
>
> Side headings are blocked at the left margin and are
> underscored. Double space before and after a side heading
> (such as the one above this paragraph).
>
>   <u>Paragraph headings</u>. These headings are indented 5
> spaces, underscored, and keyed in upper and lower case
> letters. Paragraph headings are actually part of the
> paragraph and must be followed by periods. This paragraph
> begins with a paragraph heading.

■ Tips for Word Processors

Be sure to turn on widow and orphan protection before keying the
document to make the word processing program operate within the
page break guidelines.

Business Report
(Page 1)

STANDARD FORMAT FOR A BUSINESS REPORT ↘ **1.5" (line 10)**
4 (QS)

This document is an example of a business report. Center the
title in all caps 1.5" (line 10 from the top edge of the paper).
Quadruple space after the title. (If you want to include a
subtitle, double space after the main title, key the subtitle, and
quadruple space after the subtitle.) Single space the report
body. Block the paragraphs and use 1" side margins.
2 (DS)

1"
elite 12
pica 10

1"
elite 90
pica 75

Leave a bottom margin of at least 1" (6 lines) on each page.
However, you must NOT stop more than 1.5" or 9 lines before the
bottom of the paper, except for the last page of the report, which
may end at any point on the paper.

Do not number the first page of a report; begin numbering on the
second page. On second and subsequent pages, leave a 1" top
margin by keying the page number on line 7 at the right margin
point (flush right). Double space and continue with the body.

You cannot divide the last word on a page. When dividing a
paragraph, you must leave at least 2 lines of a paragraph on the
first page and carry at least 2 lines of type to the second page.
(Remember, this is lines of type, NOT sentences!) The second line
carried to a new page may be a partial line.

     Long quotes of 4 or more lines are single spaced and indented
     5 spaces from the left margin. No quotation marks are used.
     Enumerations within a business report are formatted in the
     same way. Please refer to the *Table Within Other Documents* or
     Enumerations--Blocked pages of this reference guide for
     additional formatting information.
        2

<u>Side Headings</u>
   2

Side headings in a business report are blocked at the left margin
in upper and lower case letters. They may be bolded and underscored or keyed in a larger-size font than the rest of the report
type. They are always preceded and followed by a double space.
There is a side heading above this paragraph.

1"-2"
(6-12 blank lines)

Business Report
(Page 2)

1" (line 7) ↓ 2

1"
Paragraph headings. This type of heading is actually part of the
paragraph and must be followed by a period. Double space before   1"
it, underscore it, and use capital and and lower case letters.
This paragraph begins with a paragraph heading.

Title Page

For title pages, the goal is attractiveness. Adjust the line spacing between parts, depending on the amount of text within the parts.

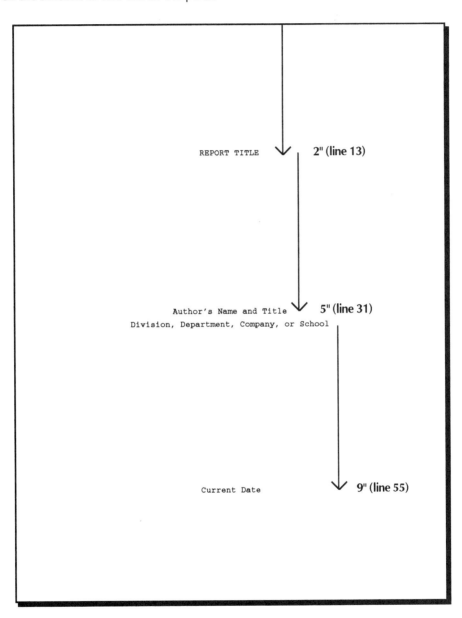

REPORT TITLE ⌄ **2" (line 13)**

Author's Name and Title ⌄ **5" (line 31)**
Division, Department, Company, or School

Current Date ⌄ **9" (line 55)**

Table of Contents

Use the same margins as the rest of the document of which the contents is a part. End the leaders 3 to 5 spaces before the right-hand column. For information on how to key leaders, see page 16.

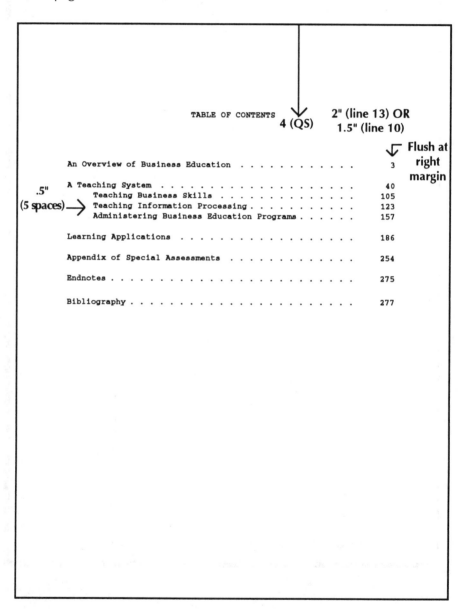

Outline Format

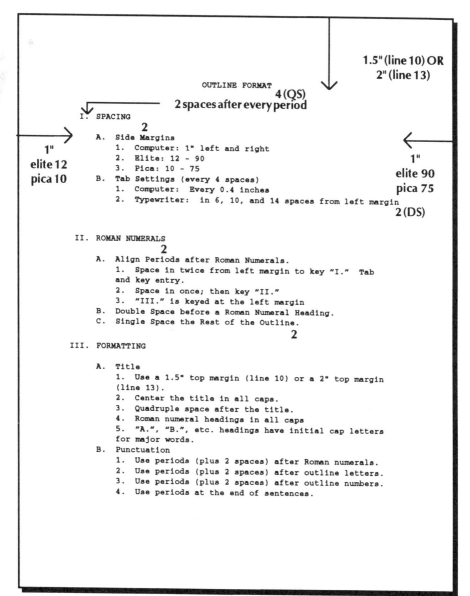

```
                              OUTLINE FORMAT
I.  SPACING

    A.  Side Margins
        1.  Computer: 1" left and right
        2.  Elite: 12 - 90
        3.  Pica: 10 - 75
    B.  Tab Settings (every 4 spaces)
        1.  Computer:  Every 0.4 inches
        2.  Typewriter:  in 6, 10, and 14 spaces from left margin


II. ROMAN NUMERALS

    A.  Align Periods after Roman Numerals.
        1.  Space in twice from left margin to key "I."  Tab
        and key entry.
        2.  Space in once; then key "II."
        3.  "III." is keyed at the left margin
    B.  Double Space before a Roman Numeral Heading.
    C.  Single Space the Rest of the Outline.

III. FORMATTING

    A.  Title
        1.  Use a 1.5" top margin (line 10) or a 2" top margin
        (line 13).
        2.  Center the title in all caps.
        3.  Quadruple space after the title.
        4.  Roman numeral headings in all caps
        5.  "A.", "B.", etc. headings have initial cap letters
        for major words.
    B.  Punctuation
        1.  Use periods (plus 2 spaces) after Roman numerals.
        2.  Use periods (plus 2 spaces) after outline letters.
        3.  Use periods (plus 2 spaces) after outline numbers.
        4.  Use periods at the end of sentences.
```

Annotations on the example:

- 1.5" (line 10) OR 2" (line 13)
- 4 (QS)
- 2 spaces after every period
- 1" elite 12 pica 10
- 2
- 1" elite 90 pica 75
- 2 (DS)
- 2
- 2

Reference List

A reference list of the sources used in preparing a document or report is placed at the end of the document or may be listed on a separate page entitled "References" or "Bibliography." (See models on pages 52-53.) Use the format shown on this page only when all the references used fit on the last page of the document.

placed into the school's library for anyone to check out. This project also demonstrated the dramatic effect of writing for an audience, since students were meticulous about their spelling, punctuation, and grammar.

The single most persuasive argument for the reading/writing workshop literacy approach is the ability to teach skills at the most teachable moment--when they're needed. If a student feels a need for a piece of knowledge, the information will stay with him better than when it's just presented as the next page in the workbook. **4 (QS)**

REFERENCES **4**

Hansen, J. "Literacy Portfolios Emerge." The Reading Teacher,
$\longrightarrow$ April 1992.
.5" (5 spaces)
Herbert, E. "Portfolios Invite Reflection from Students and
    Staff." Educational Leadership, May 1992.

Lewin, L. "Integrating Reading and Writing Strategies Using an
    Alternating Teacher-led/Student-selected Instructional
    Pattern." The Reading Teacher, April 1992.

Sudol, D. and P. Sudol. "Another Story: Putting Graves, Calkins,
    and Atwell into Practice and Perspective." Language Arts,
    April 1991.

Bibliography

A bibliography lists alphabetically the books and articles used in a report by the writer. It includes all the references used in any footnotes. It may also be called a reference page.

- Use the same side margins as the report. Begin each entry at the left margin, and indent continuation lines 0.5" or 5 spaces (just the opposite of footnote/endnote format).

- Alphabetize entries using the authors' last names. When there is no author, alphabetize by the title of the book or article. Disregard *the, a,* and *an* when alphabetizing titles. When the same author has written more than one reference, arrange those titles alphabetically.

- List pages used only for newspapers and magazine articles.

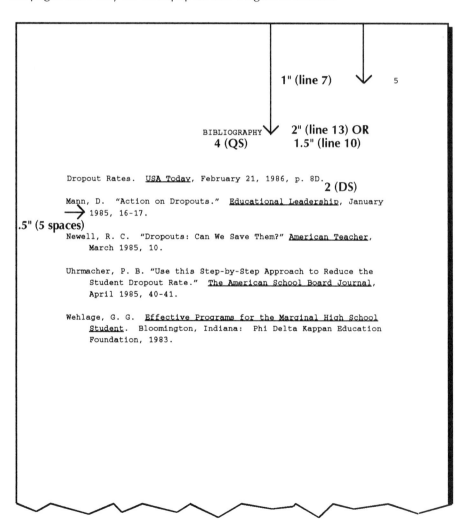

1" (line 7)   5

BIBLIOGRAPHY   2" (line 13) OR
4 (QS)   1.5" (line 10)

Dropout Rates. <u>USA Today</u>, February 21, 1986, p. 8D.
                                                                      2 (DS)

Mann, D. "Action on Dropouts." <u>Educational Leadership</u>, January
.5" (5 spaces) → 1985, 16-17.

Newell, R. C. "Dropouts: Can We Save Them?" <u>American Teacher</u>,
        March 1985, 10.

Uhrmacher, P. B. "Use this Step-by-Step Approach to Reduce the
        Student Dropout Rate." <u>The American School Board Journal</u>,
        April 1985, 40-41.

Wehlage, G. G. <u>Effective Programs for the Marginal High School
        Student</u>. Bloomington, Indiana: Phi Delta Kappan Education
        Foundation, 1983.

Internal Citations

Internal citations are modified footnotes placed in parentheses within the report body to give credit for quoted or paraphrased material. (Note the lines set off by arrows in the model). Internal citations are rapidly replacing footnotes because they are easier to key and are more efficient.

1. Internal citations show the name(s) of the author(s), the date of the publication, and the page number of the material cited, for example: (Rubin, 1993, 34). When the author's name is already mentioned in the text, only the year and page number go in the parentheses (as in the first line below).

2. All references cited are listed alphabetically by authors' last names at the end of the report or on a separate page entitled REFERENCES.

3. Internal citations eliminate the need for an endnotes page.

9

While I found Lewin's (1992, 587) literacy approach ⟵——

exciting, I worried about whether students were learning the

"nitty gritty" of writing--grammar and punctuation. Yet

research (Sudol and Sudol, 1991, 300) clearly shows that when⟵——

children encounter dilemmas and pose their own questions,

grammar skills are learned in context. Since children need

punctuation to make their writing more expressive for their

classmates, they learn it more effectively than if they do

workbook drills. Because isolated drills on punctuation have

poor transfer to actual writing, less than 10 percent of

traditionally taught students (as compared to almost 50

percent of workshop-approach students) understood that

punctuation affected the pace and inflection of language

(Calkins, 1980, 569). ⟵——

Footnotes

A footnote reference must be placed on the bottom of the page containing its quoted material. The footnote provides information about the source of the information quoted. Footnotes are numbered sequentially throughout a report with a superscript number at the exact point of reference in the text. Superscript numbers on a typewriter are keyed ½ line above the current line of type. Computer users should check their software manuals for directions in keying superscripted numbers.

1. Plan ahead to decide where to insert the line dividing the text from the footnotes. Allow 3 lines for the divider line, add 3 lines for each footnote, and add 6 lines for the bottom margin. Subtract the total lines from 66; the result is the last line on which regular text should appear.

    In the example below, the last line of text was on line 48, 18 lines before the bottom of the page:

    Divider line + 3 footnotes + Bottom margin - 66 = last line to key regular text

    3   +   9   +   6   - 66 = 48

2. Footnotes always go at the bottom of the page— EVEN WHEN it is a partial page of type.

3. If the text of the report continues to the bottom of the page, double space after the last line of type before keying the divider line.

4. Key a 1.5" long divider line (18 elite underscores; 15 pica underscores). Double space after it.

5. Indent 5 spaces. Then key the superscript number and the footnote. Each footnote entry is single spaced, with a double space between footnote entries.

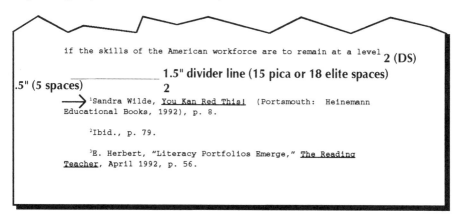

if the skills of the American workforce are to remain at a level

2 (DS)

_____ 1.5" divider line (15 pica or 18 elite spaces)

.5" (5 spaces)   2

→ ¹Sandra Wilde, You Kan Red This! (Portsmouth: Heinemann Educational Books, 1992), p. 8.

²Ibid., p. 79.

³E. Herbert, "Literacy Portfolios Emerge," The Reading Teacher, April 1992, p. 56.

■ **Tips for Word Processors**
Some word processing programs can determine where to place footnotes for you. Please refer to your specific software's instruction manual.

Endnotes

Endnotes are footnotes that are listed on a separate page at the end of a report rather than at the bottom of each page. They appear before the References or Bibliography page. Use the same margins as the report of which the endnotes are a part. Use footnote format for each entry.

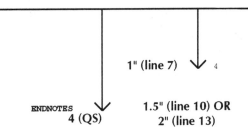

1" (line 7)

ENDNOTES
4 (QS)

1.5" (line 10) OR
2" (line 13)

[1]J. Hansen, "Integrating Reading and Writing Strategies Using an Alternating Teacher-led/Student-selected Instructional Pattern," The Reading Teacher, April 1992, p. 587.

[2]Ibid., p. 588.

[3]Nancie Atwell, In the Middle: Writing, Reading, and Learning with Adolescents, (Portsmouth: Boynton/Cook Publishers, 1987), p. 95.

[4]D. Sudol and P. Sudol, "Another Story: Putting Graves, Calkins, and Atwell into Practice and Perspective," Language Arts, April 1991, p. 300.

[5]Atwell, p. 106.

Headers

A header is text that you set to automatically print at the top (head) of each page of a document. A header may be centered or placed at the right or left margin of each page.

Some examples of common headers are
- page numbers (on only odd or even pages, or on all pages)
- document title
- date
- chapter or section title

Headers may be used on the same page as footers. Please refer to your specific software's manual for details on how to use this feature on your computer .

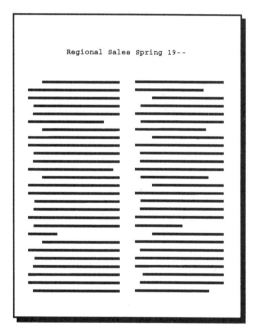

Footers

A footer is text that you set to print automatically at the bottom (foot) of each page of a document. A footer may be centered or placed at the right or left margin of each page.

Some examples of common footers are

- page numbers (on only odd or even pages, or on all pages)
- document title
- date
- chapter or section title

Footers may be used on the same page as headers. Please refer to your specific software's manual for details on how to use this feature on your computer .

Reports in Transition

The document below illustrates a report formatted with common word processor features: alternative type faces and sizes, use of bold and italic, and full justification.

RESULTS OF THE SHORTENED WORKWEEK STUDY

Introduction

Some American corporations have instituted a four-day workweek. Several of these industrial leaders have reported success based on greater productivity, enhanced employee morale, and decreased absenteeism. However, other companies who have attempted a shortened week report employee dissatisfaction due to child care problems, exhaustion from longer workdays, and the difficulty of adapting to an untraditional schedule. The success or failure of a shortened workweek depends to a large extent on the employees' desires. Therefore, a study was conducted to determine our staff's opinions of a four-day workweek.

Background of the Study

Three hundred sixty-eight company employees were randomly chosen to be surveyed from a workforce of 712.

On the survey the hourly workers were offered a continuous rotation--with four days on, then three days off throughout the year. The salaried employees would work a year-round, Monday through Thursday schedule.

Survey Synopsis

A significant finding is that *52 percent of all those surveyed wished to keep the current five-day workweek.*

Salaried/Hourly Worker Opinion. Hourly workers were strongly opposed, with only 34 percent willing to try a shortened week. Salaried workers, however, favored the four-day week; 68 percent would like to see it implemented on a three-month experimental basis.

Scheduling. Of those hourly workers who did favor a four-day workweek, most (78 percent) favored a four-day workweek as a rotation--four days on then three days off through the year. Of those salaried workers who favored a four-day workweek, most (69 percent) favored a year-round Monday through Thursday schedule.

Recommendation

Although it has some advantages, the shortened week does not have enough supporters to justify its implementation. In addition, since many of our employees work in customer support roles, they must be available the same weekdays as our customers. Shipping and receiving personnel must also be available. With so many employees fitting into these categories, it would be imprudent to adopt the four-day workweek.

■ **Tips for Word Processors**
Refer to "Page Layout Enhancements--Computers" on p. 20 for more details on using appropriate enhancements in your documents.

Section 4

Tables

Formatting Tables on Typewriters
Formatting Tables on Computers
Formatting Column Headings
Tables Within Other Documents
Ruled Tables
Tables in Landscape Mode
Tables in Transition

Format Tables—Typewriters

1. Find the longest line in each column and write the number of spaces it contains below the column.

2. Select an even number of spaces to put between columns. For narrow tables use more spaces (at least 10). For wider tables of three or more columns use fewer spaces (4, 6, or 8 spaces).

3. Add up all the spaces needed from steps 1 and 2. Divide the total spaces needed by 2. Ignore remainders!

4. Subtract the resulting number from the centerpoint (51 elite or 42 pica) to find your left margin setting. Column 1 begins here.

5. Add the number of spaces you wrote for Column 1 to the left margin setting. Then add the spaces needed between Columns 1 and 2 to this figure.

6. The resulting number is the tab setting for Column 2.

7. Add the number of spaces for Column 2 to the tab setting for Column 2. Then add the spaces needed between Columns 2 and 3 to this figure.

8. The resulting number is the tab setting for Column 3.

9. If there are additional columns, repeat this procedure to find their tab stops.

10. Clear any existing tab settings from your typewriter (refer to your typewriter's user manual for specific directions).

11. Set the left margin and tabs at the points determined by your calculations.

12. Use the **HUSH** vertical centering formula to find the line on which to begin the table. (Refer to page 10.)

13. Space down to the beginning line you determined in step 12 and center the title. If there is a subtitle, double space between it and the main title. Double space and begin the table.

14. Key the table, using your tab key to move from column to column.

    NOTE: If any number in a column contains a decimal point, all the numbers in that column must align relative to the decimal point.

Typewriter Table Example

The longest item in each column is circled in the illustration. Calculations for left margin and tab settings for this table are shown below the illustration.

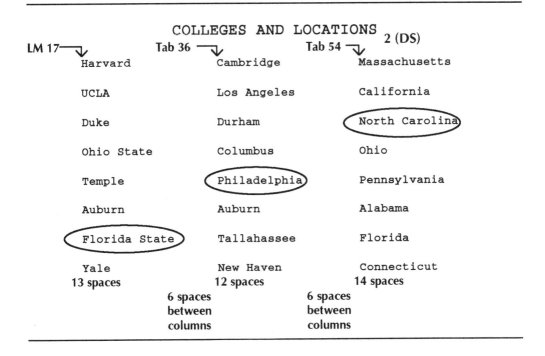

Left Margin (LM)

1. 13 + 6 + 12 + 6 + 14= 51 spaces total for table

2. 51 ÷ 2 = 25½ (drop fraction)

3. 42 (pica center) - 25 = **17 LM**

1st Tab Setting

17 LM + 13 (Column 1 spaces) + 6 (spaces between) = **36**

2nd Tab Setting

36 (1st tab) + 12 (Column 2 spaces) + 6 (spaces between)= **54**

Format Tables—Computers

1. If you do not wish to use the default margins, set the left and right margins using 1-inch to 2-inch widths.

2. Find the longest line in each column.

3. Select an even number of spaces to put between columns. For narrow tables use more spaces (at least 10). For wider tables of three or more columns use fewer spaces (4, 6, or 8 spaces).

4. Activate the centering command.

5. Key a trial line:

   - Key the longest line in the first column.
   - Press the space bar once for each blank space between columns.
   - Key the longest line in the second column.
   - Press the space bar once for each blank space between columns.
   - Key the longest line of the third column.
   - If there are additional columns, repeat these procedures.

6. Press ENTER.

7. Using your cursor to scan the trial line, note the location where each column begins. Jot the locations down on a piece of paper .

8. Delete the trial line.

9. Access the program's format instructions (or tab line), and set the tabs in the locations you wrote down from the screen. Be sure to set a decimal tab for any column that has numbers that must align.

10. After you have keyed the table, move the cursor to the very top of the document and activate the "Center Page Vertically" command so that the table is placed appropriately on the page.

11. The instructions given here will work with any computer; however, some software programs have a table feature to help you create tables. Please refer to your specific software's instruction manual.

Computer Table Example

The longest item in each column is circled in the illustration.

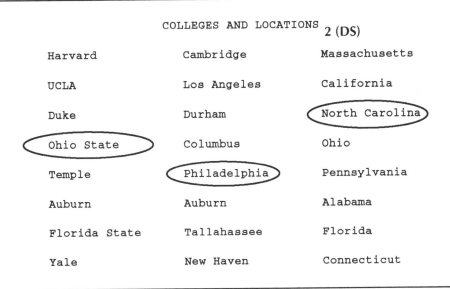

COLLEGES AND LOCATIONS 2 (DS)

Harvard	Cambridge	Massachusetts
UCLA	Los Angeles	California
Duke	Durham	North Carolina
Ohio State	Columbus	Ohio
Temple	Philadelphia	Pennsylvania
Auburn	Auburn	Alabama
Florida State	Tallahassee	Florida
Yale	New Haven	Connecticut

To prepare this table, first turn on centering and key this trial line:

Ohio State 1/2/3/4/5/6 Philadelphia 1/2/3/4/5/6 North Carolina

**Press space bar
once for each
blank space**

Set the tabs as indicated by the trial line. (Be sure to delete the trial line after you've determined your tab settings!)

Blocked Column Headings

Blocked column headings are easy to do and are gaining in popularity. Blocked column headings look best when they are close in length to the longest lines in the columns beneath them (as shown here):

```
                        SALES CONTEST WINNERS
                                2 (DS)
        Sales Representative        Total Sales        District
                                         2
        Michael Patterson         $189,750          Northwest

        Jamie Auberger             176,850          Southeast

        Julie Wytiora              166,500          Southwest

        Arnold VanHooten           166,350          Northeast

        Debra Finlayson            143,575          Central
```

1. If the column heading is the longest line in that column, use it in your trial line or calculations.

2. Determine the tab settings for the table (based on the directions given for your equipment).

3. Blocked column headings begin at the tabs set for the table.

4. All of the information in each column is keyed at the tab settings.

5. Always double space before and after the column headings (even if the body of the table is single spaced).

Centered Column
Headings

MAIN HEADING (TITLE) FOR TABLE 2 (DS)

Secondary Heading (Subtitle) for Table 2

<u>These</u>	<u>Are</u>	<u>Column</u>	<u>Headings</u>
This is how	the	body of	the table
aligns under	the	columns.	

_2_

To center each heading over its column:

1. Find the longest line in the column. If the longest line is the column heading, refer to "Column Headings Wider than Column" on page 70.

2. Subtract the number of spaces in the column heading from the number of spaces in the longest line.

3. Divide by 2. Ignore fractions!

4. The resulting number is the number of spaces to indent the heading from the margin or tab stop for that column.

5. Repeat steps 1 through 4 for each column heading in the table.

6. Always double space before and after the column heading (even if the body of the table is single spaced).

> ■ **Tips for Word Processors**
> It is easiest to leave a blank line for the column headings. After the table is completely keyed, return to this blank line and center the column headings over the columns using the procedures outlined above.

Centered Column
Headings Example

In the example below, the longest line in each column is circled.

ELMRIDGE ACADEMY

2 **(DS)**

Junior Varsity Basketball

2

<u>Date</u>   <u>Versus</u>   <u>Site</u>

2

```
January 27         Elton-Lynchfield      Home
February 10        Portsmouth            Away
February 19        Green Forest          Home
February 28        Rushford              Away
March 9            St. Benedict          Away
```

February 10	Elton-Lynchfield	Home
11 spaces	16 spaces	4 spaces
- 4 (**Date**)	- 6 (**Versus**)	-4 (**Site**)
7÷2 = 3½	10÷2 = **5**	0
(drop fraction)		
Indent **3** spaces and key column heading	Indent **5** spaces from from the tab and key column heading	Put the column heading at the tab stop

69

Column Headings
Wider than Columns

When column headings are wider than the longest line in the column, you must center the columns below the column headings.

```
            MAIN HEADING (TITLE) FOR TABLE
                      2 (DS)
        Secondary Heading (Subtitle) for Table
                                             2

These Column Headings           Are the Longest Item in Column
                                                             2

    Therefore, the              columns of the table are
    centered under              the column headings.
```

To center each column under its heading:

1. Use the heading as the longest line when determining the left margin and the tab settings for the table.

2. Subtract the number of spaces in the longest line in the column from the number of spaces in the column heading.

3. Divide by 2. Ignore fractions!

4. The resulting number is the number of spaces to indent the column from the margin or tab set for that column heading. All items in the column begin here.

5. Repeat steps 2 through 4 for each column where the heading is the longest line.

6. Always double space before and after the column heading (even when the body of the table is single spaced).

> ■ **Tips for Word Processors**
> Generate TWO trial lines: one using the column heading as the longest line and another with the longest line in each column. Then be sure to note all the tab settings with your cursor and delete both trial lines before keying the table.

Wide Column
Headings Example

In the example below, the longest line in each column is circled.

WORST NATURAL DISASTERS

2 (DS)

In Recorded American History

2

<u>Type of Disaster</u>	<u>Fatalities</u>
Earthquake	500
Fire	1,200
Hurricane	6,000
Tornado	792

<u>Type of Disaster</u>	<u>Fatalities</u>
16 spaces	10 spaces
<u>-10</u> spaces (Earthquake)	<u>- 5</u> spaces (6,000)
6 ÷ 2= **3**	5 ÷ 2 = **2 ½** (ignore fraction)
Indent column **3** spaces	Indent column **2** spaces
from column heading	from column heading

Table Within a Document

Follow these steps to key a table inside another document (such as a report, memo, or letter).

1. To set it off from the main document, double space before and after the table.

2. Use the same line spacing for the table body as for the rest of the document.

3. Center the table within the side margins of the document. NEVER extend a table outside the margins of the main document!

4. Refer to page 62 or page 64 for formatting instructions for your machine (computer or typewriter).

5. Never split a table onto two pages. If the table cannot fit entirely on one page, put it at the top of the next page and refer to it in the text with a statement like "See Table 3.2."

Many taxpayers feel that the cost of education is astronomically high. Yet compared to elsewhere in the state, the cost to educate a pupil in our county's schools is a bargain. The table below shows in descending order the amount area districts spent on each student during the last academic year. Since they only attend for a half day, each kindergartner counts as a half pupil.

COST PER STUDENT

School District	AMOUNT	
Foxworth Central	$7,369	**Center table**
Herrington	7,223	**within**
Blossom-Keyes	6,907	**document**
Kingsley	6,612	**margins**
Gorton-Red Creek	6,410	

Considering that the Gastonburg City School District spent $10,786 on each student during the last academic year, our regional schools are doing an excellent job of holding costs down while still providing a quality educational experience for our children.

Ruled Table Format

1. You will need to first determine the proper left margin and tab settings for the table. See page 62 or page 64.

2. On a typewriter, use the **HUSH** formula to determine the line on which to begin the table. On a computer use the "Center Page Vertically" feature AFTER you've completed the table and returned the cursor to the top of the document.

3. The phrase "one comes before two" will help you remember the spacing used in a ruled table. SINGLE SPACE before keying a ruled line, and always DOUBLE SPACE after keying a ruled line.

4. Begin the rules at the exact left margin and end the rules at the exact right margin.

5. Mark reference notes and the table parts to which they refer with an asterisk (as shown below). Place the reference notes a double space below the last ruled line.

6. Do not indent one-line notes; however, notes with two or more lines may be indented 5 spaces (like footnotes in a report).

7. You may make any ruled table into a boxed table:

   Typewriter users: Draw vertical lines halfway between columns by inserting the table sideways into a typewriter and keying a solid line of underscores.

   Computer users: Many programs now offer a line draw feature that can insert vertical lines for you. Please refer to your specific software's instruction manual.

TERRITORY MANAGERS **2 (DS)**

Southwestern Region*

Name	City	
Kate Atkinson	San Francisco	2
Osami Kinoshita	Houston	
Paul Littlebear	Dallas	
Tien Sheng	Ft. Worth	
Margarita Valdes	El Paso	

*As of February 9, 19--.

Formatting Tables/Landscape Mode (Paper Sideways)

Sometimes you will need to prepare a table that is too wide to fit on the 8.5" width of standard paper. In this case, turn the paper sideways so that you can use the 11" width.

Typewriter users: The only adjustment you have to make is to use the different centerpoint in your calculations. Follow the directions given on page 62 to format your table properly.

Computer users: Follow the steps indicated for your software for landscape mode *before* you set up the table. Then follow the directions given on page 64 to format your table properly.

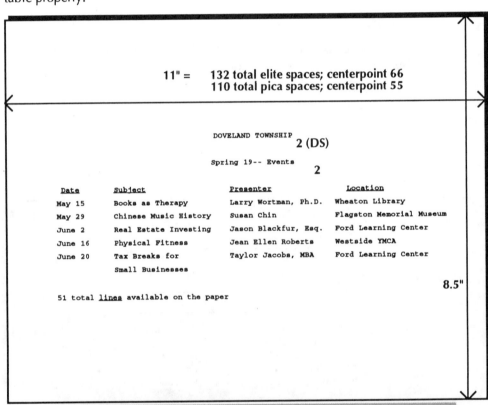

11" = 132 total elite spaces; centerpoint 66
       110 total pica spaces; centerpoint 55

DOVELAND TOWNSHIP 2 (DS)

Spring 19-- Events 2

Date	Subject	Presenter	Location
May 15	Books as Therapy	Larry Wortman, Ph.D.	Wheaton Library
May 29	Chinese Music History	Susan Chin	Flagston Memorial Museum
June 2	Real Estate Investing	Jason Blackfur, Esq.	Ford Learning Center
June 16	Physical Fitness	Jean Ellen Roberts	Westside YMCA
June 20	Tax Breaks for Small Businesses	Taylor Jacobs, MBA	Ford Learning Center

8.5"

51 total lines available on the paper

■ **Tips for Word Processors**

Since some printers do not possess the ability to print in the landscape mode, be sure to check with your software AND your printer to see if you can print in landscape mode. If you cannot do it on your computer, key the table on two separate pages using the regular 8.5" width, then tape them together (on the back), and use a photocopier to reduce the table to fit on a standard sheet of paper.

Tables in Transition

CIRCULATION OF TOP 10 AMERICAN & CANADIAN MAGAZINES	
Magazine	Circulation
Reader's Digest	17,666,947
TV Guide	16,687,908
National Geographic	10,890,660
Better Homes & Gardens	8,005,311
Family Circle	5,461,786
Good Housekeeping	5,152,245
McCall's	5,088,686
Ladies' Home Journal	5,038,297
Woman's Day	4,705,288
Teen	4,339,029

Source: *The 1991 Information Please Almanac*, p. 297.

■ Tips for Word Processors

Some software packages offer a "Table" feature that will set up a table for you. Most of the programs that offer this special feature also offer shading and horizontal and vertical rulings (lines).

One of the most helpful aspects of the "Table" feature is that it automatically adjusts the entire table when you add or delete information. For more details, please refer to your specific software's instruction manual.

Other Documents

Agenda

Itinerary

Resume

News Release

Traditional Minutes

Action Minutes

Invoice

Purchase Order

Agenda

Refer to page 16 for directions on how to key leaders. Enumerations for agenda items are optional.

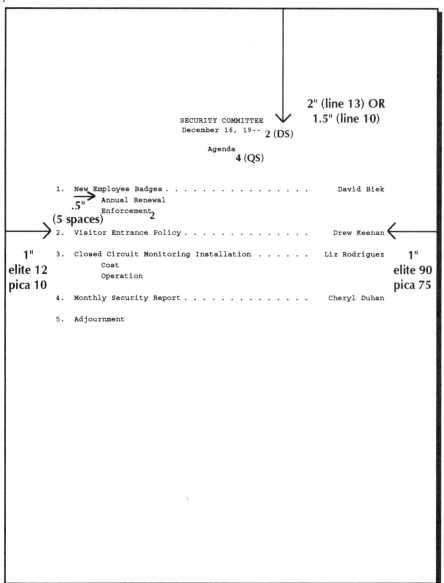

SECURITY COMMITTEE
December 16, 19-- **2 (DS)**

2" (line 13) OR 1.5" (line 10)

Agenda
4 (QS)

1. New Employee Badges . . . .   David Biek
   .5" Annual Renewal
   (5 spaces) Enforcement **2**

2. Visitor Entrance Policy . . . .   Drew Keenan

1"
elite 12
pica 10

3. Closed Circuit Monitoring Installation . . . . . .   Liz Rodriguez

   Cost
   Operation

1"
elite 90
pica 75

4. Monthly Security Report . . . .   Cheryl Duhan

5. Adjournment

■ Tips for Word Processors
You can use the computer's right flush feature to properly align the names at the right margin. Please refer to your specific software's instruction manual.

Itinerary

Date lines may be prepared in cap and lowercase and bold (no underscore), if you prefer. Align the colons in the times listed at the left margin.

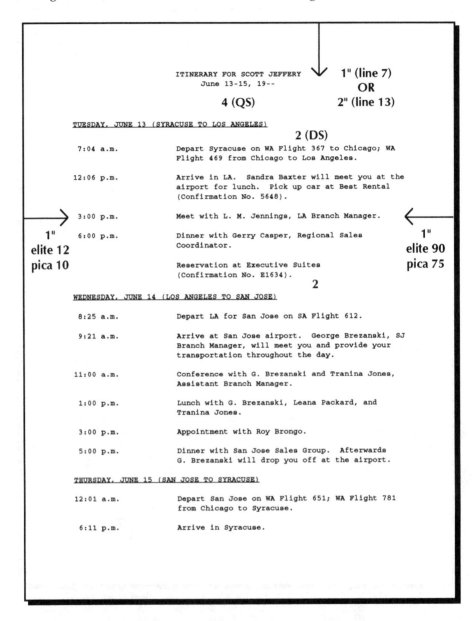

ITINERARY FOR SCOTT JEFFERY
June 13-15, 19--

1" (line 7)
OR
2" (line 13)

4 (QS)

TUESDAY, JUNE 13 (SYRACUSE TO LOS ANGELES)

2 (DS)

7:04 a.m.   Depart Syracuse on WA Flight 367 to Chicago; WA
               Flight 469 from Chicago to Los Angeles.

12:06 p.m.   Arrive in LA. Sandra Baxter will meet you at the
               airport for lunch. Pick up car at Best Rental
               (Confirmation No. 5648).

3:00 p.m.   Meet with L. M. Jennings, LA Branch Manager.

6:00 p.m.   Dinner with Gerry Casper, Regional Sales
               Coordinator.

               Reservation at Executive Suites
               (Confirmation No. E1634).

2

1"
elite 12
pica 10

1"
elite 90
pica 75

WEDNESDAY, JUNE 14 (LOS ANGELES TO SAN JOSE)

8:25 a.m.   Depart LA for San Jose on SA Flight 612.

9:21 a.m.   Arrive at San Jose airport. George Brezanski, SJ
               Branch Manager, will meet you and provide your
               transportation throughout the day.

11:00 a.m.   Conference with G. Brezanski and Tranina Jones,
               Assistant Branch Manager.

1:00 p.m.   Lunch with G. Brezanski, Leana Packard, and
               Tranina Jones.

3:00 p.m.   Appointment with Roy Brongo.

5:00 p.m.   Dinner with San Jose Sales Group. Afterwards
               G. Brezanski will drop you off at the airport.

THURSDAY, JUNE 15 (SAN JOSE TO SYRACUSE)

12:01 a.m.   Depart San Jose on WA Flight 651; WA Flight 781
               from Chicago to Syracuse.

6:11 p.m.   Arrive in Syracuse.

Basic Resume Format

JASMINE MENDIOLA
372 Dalston Lane
Oak Valley, NY 12234
(706) 685-3859

1" (line 7) minimum

4 (QS)

Career Objective

2 (DS)

A challenging office management position that involves interaction with people and opportunity for advancement.

2

Skills

1"
elite 12
pica 10

Microsoft Word for Windows and WordPerfect for Windows word processing, machine transcription, shorthand, filing, bookkeeping, and switchboard operation. Keying speed: 70 wpm.

1"
elite 90
pica 75

Employment Experience

Administative assistant. State Department of Vocational Education, March 1989-present. Work for rehabilitation counselors aiding mentally, physically, and emotionally disabled adults seeking employment. Use Mac computer to do machine transcription of letters and caseload reports. Greet clients, maintain office database, and operate switchboard.

Secretary. State Department of Labor, June 1986-March 1989. Worked for ten investigators. Keyed reports, letters, and forms. Prepared travel vouchers, maintained files, kept detailed monetary records, handled cash, and was responsible for the department's inventory.

Office clerk. J. R. Michael Company, August 1983-May 1986. Arranged travel accommodations and business conferences, took dictation, prepared documents and forms, maintained files, performed recordkeeping duties, and was responsible for the department's quarterly inventory.

Education

Graduated from Franklin High School 1983.

References

Furnished upon request.

News Release

This document is prepared to notify newspapers and and other media of newsworthy organizational events. The symbol ### is centered a double space below the last line of text and indicates the end of the news release.

St. Lawrence Mental Health Center
567 Connelly Road
Buffalo, NY 14201-4235
716-839-4821

News Release   For Release: Upon receipt
                                                Contact: Shirley
Sorghum

                                                               716-275-3882   **4 (QS)**

   BUFFALO, NY, February 28, 19--. The St. Lawrence Mental   **2 (DS)**

Health Clinic is constructing a new, larger facility at 4391 West

Ridge Road to serve its many clients in the Buffalo area.

   The Clinic, currently located at 567 Connelly Boulevard,

specializes in the prevention and treatment of mental disorders.

1"
elite 12   It also offers educational services and support groups for   **1"**
pica 10   families of patients. Dr. Arnaldo Alvarez, director of the   **elite 90**
                                                                                pica 75

Clinic, explains: "Since there is a great deal of ignorance

regarding mental illnesses, one part of our mission is to en-

lighten society regarding the causes, prevention, and treatment of

such diseases as depression, schizophrenia, and neurosis. The

fact is that mental illness can strike anyone at any time."

Ebony Bostwick, spokeswoman for the Clinic adds, "Moving to a

modernized center in the heart of the city makes our organization

more accessible, which not only benefits our clients but the

general public as well."

   The ground-breaking ceremony for the Clinic will be held next

Friday; construction is scheduled for completion by this October.

In addition to the many services available, the Clinic is already

slated to be the future site of several mental health conventions.

                                                                              2

                    ###

Traditional Minutes

MINUTES OF THE JULY MEETING
Employee Recreation Department

1" (line 7) OR
2" (line 13)

2 (DS)

July 31, 19--

4 (QS)

Attendance 2

**1"
elite 12
pica 10**

The July meeting of the Employee Recreation Department of Polymer
Plastics Corporation was held on July 30, 19--, in Conference
Room D. The meeting began at 1:15 p.m. and adjourned at 3:30 p.m.
Department Manager Trishana Bloise chaired the meeting. All members
except Carolyn Styles and John Barry were present. 2

**1"
elite 90
pica 75**

Approval of Minutes

The secretary read the minutes of the June meeting. They were
approved without change.

Unfinished Business

Juan Miranda gave an update on the survey he is conducting regarding employee interest in a variety of possible future activities.
He plans to have accumulated all the data necessary for a full
report by August 5 and will announce the final results at the
August meeting.

New Business

Vernon Brown discussed the need for planning a more aggressive and
timely bulletin board campaign to let employees know well in advance when activities are scheduled. He has received several complaints from workers who want to participate in our programs but
don't have enough prior notice to arrange for child care.

Helen McAllister distributed the Annual Participation Tally, which
shows a substantial increase in employee participation in recrea-
tional programs last year.

Respectfully submitted,

Miguel Diego, Secretary

Action Minutes

EMPLOYEE RECREATION DEPARTMENT JULY MEETING   ↓ **1.5" (line 10)**
July 31, 19--
2 (DS)
Action Minutes

4 (QS)

Presiding: Trishana Bloise, Department Manager
2
Participants: All members except Carolyn Styles and John Barry
2
Juan Miranda gave an update on the survey he is conducting
regarding employee interest in a variety of possible future
activities. He plans to have accumulated all the data necessary
for a full report by August 5 and will announce the final results
at the August meeting.

Vernon Brown discussed the need for planning a more aggressive and
timely bulletin board campaign to let employees know well in
advance when activities are scheduled. He has received several
complaints from workers who want to participate in our programs
but don't have enough prior notice to arrange for child care.

Helen McAllister distributed the Annual Participation Tally, which
shows a substantial increase in employee participation in recre-
ational programs last year.

The August department meeting is scheduled for August 28.

1"
elite 12
pica 10

1"
elite 90
pica 75

Formatting Invoices

An invoice is used when your organization bills a customer for products they purchased from your organization. Information on preprinted forms (such as invoices) is usually filled in using a typewriter.

1. Set the left margin so that items in the "Quantity" column are approximately centered.

2. Set your first tab to align the address block TWO spaces to the right of the vertical rule preceding the "Description" column. The all-caps address information (in "Sold To:" box) will also be keyed at the first tab.

3. Set a tab to align the information at the top right TWO spaces to the right of the printed colons. You can frequently key the "Unit Price" information also at this tab.

4. Set a tab (decimal tab if your typewriter has this feature) for the "Total" column to accommodate the length of the total amount due.

5. Key the entries a double space below the printed horizontal line. Single space each item; DS between items.

6. Underline the last amount in the "Total" column, extending the underline over the longest item in the column (usually the bottom total number). Do not key dollar signs on an invoice.

State-of-the-Art Computer Services
1579 Eleanor Road
Topeka, KS 66203-4700
913-662-8593 — **Tab**

Sold To:

OUR COMPUTER CLUB
461 ASTELARE AVENUE
RALEIGH NC 27601-6814

2 spaces INVOICE

Date: January 16, 19--
Invoice No.: 16667349A
Order No.:   EH343151
Shipped by: APS
Terms: 2/10, net 30

Quantity	Description/Stock No.	Unit Price	Total
	2 (DS)		
5	Hard disk drives, Cat. No. 586	1,159 19	5,795 95
5	Laser printers, Cat. No.994	384 60	1,923 00
5	EZ Touch keyboards, Cat. No. 345	275 15	1,375 75
5	Low dot pitch screens, Cat. No. 146	1,225 00	6,125 00
			15,219 70

Center

■ **Tips for Word Processors**
Most businesses are beginning to use templates instead of traditional preprinted forms. With a word processing template, you create a standard format for your organization's forms (such as invoices). Each time you need the form, you bring it up on your computer screen, fill in the information, and print out an original copy. Please refer to your specific software's instruction manual.

Formatting Purchase Orders

A purchase order is a request by your company to order merchandise from another organization. Information on preprinted forms (such as purchase orders) is usually filled in using a typewriter.

1. Set the left margin so that items in the "Quantity" column are approximately centered.

2. Set your first tab to align the address block TWO spaces to the right of the vertical rule preceding the "Description" column. The all-caps address information (in "To:" box) and the item description will also be keyed at the first tab.

3. Set a tab to align the information at the top right TWO spaces to the right of the printed colons. You can frequently key the "Unit Price" column also at this tab.

4. Set a tab (decimal tab if your typewriter has this feature) for the "Total" column to accommodate the length of the total amount due.

5. Key the entries a double space (DS) below the printed horizontal line. Single space each item; DS between items.

6. Underline the last amount in the "Total" column, extending the line over the longest item in the column (usually the bottom total number). Do not key dollar signs on a purchase order.

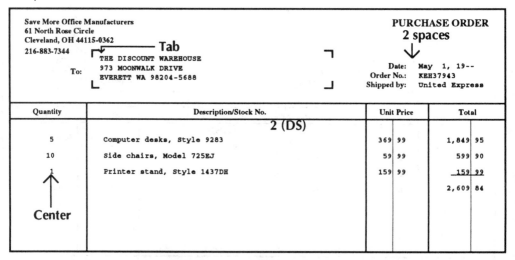

Save More Office Manufacturers
61 North Rose Circle
Cleveland, OH 44115-0362
216-883-7344

PURCHASE ORDER
2 spaces

Tab

THE DISCOUNT WAREHOUSE
To: 973 MOONWALK DRIVE
EVERETT WA 98204-5688

Date: May 1, 19--
Order No.: KEH37943
Shipped by: United Express

Quantity	Description/Stock No.	Unit Price		Total	
	2 (DS)				
5	Computer desks, Style 9283	369	99	1,849	95
10	Side chairs, Model 725EJ	59	99	599	90
1	Printer stand, Style 1437DH	159	99	159	99
				2,609	84

Center

> **■ Tips for Word Processors**
> Most businesses are beginning to use templates instead of traditional preprinted forms. With a word processing template, you create a standard format for your organization's forms (such as purchase orders). Each time you need the form, you bring it up on your computer screen, fill in the information, and print out an original copy. Please refer to your specific software's instruction manual.

Communication Skills Appendix

Number Expression

Proofreader's Marks

Punctuation Usage

Symbols: Meaning and Usage

Line Break Rules

Word Division Rules

Confusing Words

Capitalization Rules

Number Expression Guides

Always use words for

1. Numbers one to ten
   There are six girls in the car.

2. Fractions in a sentence (not mixed with whole numbers)
   At least one fifth of our clients were unsatisfied.

3. Ordinals
   They are celebrating their thirty-third anniversary.

4. First word in a sentence
   Sixty-two dogs were entered in the show.

5. Street names (first - tenth)
   He used to live at 43 Fifth Avenue.

6. House number one
   Ship it to One Parkside Drive.

7. Approximate or large round numbers
   Amost three hundred people joined in the march.

Always use figures for

1. Numbers 11 and greater
   Put the 12 boxes over there.

2. Mixed numbers
   Our new home sits on 7 1/2 wooded acres.

3. Ages
   Sue Feathers, 28, expects her baby in March.

4. Measurements
   3 feet, 7 pounds, 5 quarts, 3 grams

5. Money/Percentages
   $1.98, 23 cents, $700, 67 percent, 36%, 0.6 percent

6. Time/Dates
   7 a.m.; 11:15 p.m.; 3 o'clock; May 15, 1997; 7/3/96; 2 July 1998

7. Decimals
   7.8, 0.015

8. Numbers preceded by a descriptor
   Room 16B, Volume 7, Invoice 4673

9. Addresses (house numbers 2 & up; street names 11 & up)
   14 34th Boulevard, 769 West 43 Avenue

Express related numbers as the LARGEST number is expressed:

**Only 3 of the 148 students refused to come to the ceremony.
Of the 17 documents, 10 were saved and 7 were destroyed.**

Proofreader's Marks

Meaning	Symbol	Usage
Capitalize	≡ *or* c a p	b̲≡̲ *or* b c a p
Close up	⌒	Mr. Tren⌒ton
Delete	ℰ	propₑ̸erty
Insert	∧	measurᵉment
Insert a space	⧣ *or* /	WandaOrtiz *or* Wanda⧸Ortiz
Insert comma	⌄,	however⌄I am
Insert a period	⨀	Please wait⨀
Change to lowercase	/ *or* ℓc	Please put the D̸esk here. Please put the ℓc D̸esk here.
New paragraph	¶	¶Now is the time to do it.
Transpose (reverse position)	∼ *or* tR	a⌇ction *or* at^{tR}cion
Ignore the correction	STET	Do not shout at me! ^{STET}
Move right	⊐	This⟧ is the right time.
Move left	⊏	⊏How is he?
Spell it out	⬭ *or* SP	^{SP}NY *or* (NY)
Align (line up)	‖	‖9. Make sure that the ‖10. Periods align.
Move down	⌊___⌋	⌊That's⌋ not right.
Move up; raise	⌈‾‾⌉	Please⌈fix⌉this.
Insert apostrophe	⌄'	Sharon˅' coat
Insert quotes	⌄''	"It's here!⌄''he said.
Underline or italicize	_____	War and Peace

Punctuation Usage

Use an APOSTROPHE (')

1. To show ownership:

   one person ownership . . . . the woman's shoes
   people's individual ownership . . . . several boys' jeans
   joint ownership . . . . Bonnie and Bill's children
   separate ownership . . . . dentist's and doctor's bills

2. To abbreviate feet and minutes on tables or forms (use quotes for inches and seconds) :

   The board was 3'4" wide by 12'7" long.
   He finished the race with a time of 7'11".

Use a COLON (:)

1. To introduce a list, a question, or a long quote:

   These are my favorite artists: Picasso, da Vinci, and Rembrandt.
   This is the question that counts: Did you get the money?
   In his book, <u>The Ragged Wind</u>, Jose Fernandez wrote:
       "It was not a familiar scene to her; in fact, it did not
       feel like a homecoming at all. Even the front porch with
       her beloved squeaky glider seemed different."

Use a COMMA (,)

1. To separate an introductory clause (a phrase that cannot stand alone as a complete sentence) from the remainder of the sentence (which could stand alone and is underlined in the examples below). Introductory clauses often begin with *if, when,* or *as.*

   When you leave, <u>please close the door behind you.</u>
   If you do not pay by the due date, <u>there will be a late</u>
   <u>charge</u>.
   As soon as I receive a copy, <u>I will forward it to you</u>.

2. To set off nonessential (grammatically unnecessary) words, such as *however, of course,* and *therefore,* from the rest of the sentence. A person's name is nonessential when you are directly addressing that person.

   This information, of course, is strictly confidential.
   Therefore, please send your check to us immediately.
   I am, however, grateful that you notified me.
   It is a pleasure, Mr. Grant, to serve you.
   Do you still have that book I lent to you, Scott?

3. To set off words that restate, identify, or explain something. The words inside the commas describe the previous word(s). Dates, addresses, and titles may fall in this category.

   Our sales manager, Lisa Stanton, will retire in September.
   On Wednesday, January 16, 1991, the Persian Gulf War began.

```
Sue's hometown, Appleton, Nebraska, is located on a lake.
Two conditions, wind and snow, made driving hazardous.
```

4. With *which* or *who* clauses that are unnecessary to the sense of the sentence:

```
The house, which is in a desirable area, is priced at
$205,900.
Ed Daly, who is the district manager, had a heart attack
today.
```

These *which* and *who* clauses are necessary to the sense of the sentence; therefore, use NO comma:

```
Please tell me which suit you prefer.
Is that the girl who looks like Mary?
```

5. To separate two independent clauses that are joined by one of the following conjunctions: *but, and, nor, for, or, yet.* The clauses on both sides of the conjunction could stand alone as separate sentences.

```
I saw him in May, but I haven't seen him since then.
Send for your free sample, and try it in your own home.
```

Do not use a comma unless both clauses separated by the conjunction are independent:

```
I spoke with him in June but haven't heard from him since
then.
The baby was hungry but had just been fed.
```

6. To separate two adjectives that describe the same noun. (In these cases, the word *and* could be inserted in place of the comma.)

```
It was a cold, windy day.
We provide fast, efficient handling for your packages.
```

Do not use a comma when *and* cannot be inserted between the the words and still make sense.

```
Simply fill out the enclosed yellow registration card.
The blouse was in an attractive silver gift box.
```

7. To separate words or phrases in a series of three or more items:

```
Food, shelter, and clothing are the basic necessities of
life.
Go to the corner, turn left, then take a left at the first
light.
```

8. To set off a direct quote (the actual words spoken or written by someone else):

```
"Cancel the order," Robert demanded.
Barb said, "Answer me right now!"
"The trouble is," she sighed, "I can't afford to pay my
bills."
```

Use a DASH (--)

A dash is made of two hyphens keyed together without any spaces. Some software has the capability to make an unbroken dash.

1. To provide more emphasis than commas:
   ```
   The icy road--which resembled a skating rink--was treacherous.
   ```

2. To introduce the author's name following a direct quote:
   ```
   "To be or not to be; that is the question."--Shakespeare
   ```

Use an EXCLAMATION MARK (!):

1. To provide emphasis:
   ```
   What a gorgeous day!
   ```

Use a HYPHEN (-)

Use these guides to determine when to use hyphens as punctuation--not when to break words at line endings.

1. When two adjectives are used as a single unit to describe the noun that follows them:
   ```
   I need an up-to-date bulletin.
   The postage-paid envelope is for your response.
   The well-known singer was rushed to the hospital.
   ```

2. After each word in a series that describes the same noun:
   ```
   We took the first-, second-, and third-grade students on the
   field trip to the zoo.
   ```

3. In numbers over 20 that are expressed in words:
   ```
   More than seventy-five candidates were selected last night.
   ```

4. To separate a married woman's maiden name from her husband's last name:
   ```
   Suzanne Grahan-Smith
   Dr. Louise Farley-Klement
   ```

5. To always separate *self*:
   ```
   self-conscious
   self-assured
   ```

6. Never hyphenate adverbs (words ending with *ly*):
   ```
   highly honored guest
   really special dinner
   ```

Use PARENTHESES ()

1. To enclose explanatory material:
   ```
   The statistics (see Table 2.2) prove this point as well.
   ```

2. To enclose identifying numbers in a run-in list:
   ```
   Please include the following items: (1) flashlight, (2)
   sleeping bags, (3) can opener, and (4) matches.
   ```

Use a PERIOD (.)

1. To end a complete sentence:

   That's definitely my favorite movie.

2. At the end of a polite request (when you you expect action, not an answer):

   Will you please confirm this reservation immediately.

Use a QUESTION MARK (?)

1. To end a question (you expect a reply, not action):

   What day is the Spring Formal?

Use QUOTATION MARKS ("):

1. For direct quotes (conversation):

   Inga said, "I'll arrive by 10 a.m."

2. For special (coined) phrases:

   This has definitely been a "Murphy's Law" day for me!

3. For parts of a published or unpublished work (not books):

   Read "How to Feed a Picky Eater" in <u>Today's Parents</u> magazine.
   His thesis, "The Psychological Effects of Television Viewing on Children 2-10", may be published next June.

4. As an abbreviation for inches and seconds on tables or forms (use an apostrophe for feet and minutes):

   The board was 3'4" wide by 12'7" long.
   He finished the race with a time of 7'11".

Use a SEMICOLON (;)

1. To separate two closely related complete sentences that are not joined by a conjunction:

   Don't lose the coupon; it's worth $5 off your next order.
   Bring warm clothing; Rochester is quite cold in February.

2. To separate the individual items of a series that have internal commas:

   His itinerary includes stops in: Dallas, Texas; New Orleans, Louisiana; Atlanta, Georgia; and Tampa, Florida.
   Our guest panelists are Ted Baldwin, PSN Industries; Kirk Anson, Walsh Enterprises; and Alicia Reyes, Computer Associates.

3. To separate two closely related complete sentences that are joined by a conjunctive adverb (such as *however, consequently,* and *therefore*):

   He preferred outdoor work; therefore, he was willing to take a pay cut.
   The skating rink closes to the public at noon; however, you may reserve it in advance for special afternoon events.

Symbols: Meaning and Usage

SYMBOL	MEANING	USAGE
#	Before a number means number. After a number means pound.	#3265-90 32# of nails
$	Money	$14.52
%	Percent sign (used ONLY in statistical forms or tables).	62.5%
&	Ampersand means *and*.	Perez & Sons
*	Asterisk used to refer the reader to another location.	*See page 8.
-	One - means a hyphenated word.	up-to-date
--	Two -- means a dash.	Wait--don't go!
____	Underscore identifies a published work or highlights information.	Let's read <u>Lassie</u>.
( )	Parentheses used to set off information from surrounding text.	We'll come soon (I hope!)
{ }	Brackets used to set off numbers in mathematical formulas.	6{4 x 5} + {9 - 1}
'	Apostrophe used to show possession. Apostrophe used to show contraction.	Katy's coat shouldn't
"	Quotation marks surround conversation.	"Hi!" "What's up?"
!	Exclamation mark shows excitement.	Stop! Don't move!
@	Means *at*. NEVER used in documents.	6 @ $2 = $12
=	Equal sign used in mathematical equations.	567 - 324 = 243
+	Addition sign used in mathematical equations.	65 + 34 = 99
x	Lowercase x used as multiplication.	What is 7 x 8?
-	Use single hyphen for subtraction.	10 - 5 = 5
Division	Colon intersected by a hyphen (use overstrike feature on a computer).	130 ÷ 10 = 13
/	Slash used to separate parts of a date. Slash used to separate words.	9/29/97 his/her choice
. . .	Ellipsis used to show missing words.	it . . . also

Roman Numerals	Use capitals I, V , X, L, C, D, & M.	Chapter XIV
Feet & inches	Apostrophe = feet; quotes = seconds	Sue is 5'8".
Minutes & seconds	Apostrophe = hours; quotes = minutes	Time: 6'25"
Superscript	Letter or number placed above line of type.	$8^2 = 64$
Subscript	Letter or number placed below line of type.	H_2O is water.
° (Degree sign)	Place lowercase o as a superscript. (Use the degree sign on a computer.)	$12°C$

Line Break Rules

The rules below pertain to groups of words/numbers that cannot be separated onto two different lines. Refer to pages 98-99 (Word Division Rules) for rules to follow to divide individual words at the ends of lines.

1. A person's courtesy title and first name must remain on the same line.

    Incorrect: **Ms./Rosa Cortinez**   Correct: **Ms. Rosa/Cortinez**

2. If there are only two parts to a person's name, keep them on the same line.

    Incorrect: **Dr./Lopez**   Correct: **Dr. Lopez**
    Incorrect: **Lincoln/Glover**   Correct: **Lincoln Glover**

3. A month and date must stay together. When no date is given, the month and year must stay together.

    Incorrect: **March/9, 1996**   Correct: **March 9,/1996**
    Incorrect: **April/1998**   Correct: **April 1998**

4. Do not begin a line of type with a punctuation mark.

    Incorrect: **Please wait**   Correct: **Henry please wait--**
    --I want you to stay!   **I want you to stay!**

5. A number must stay with its descriptor.

    Incorrect: **8:33/a.m., 7/o'clock** Correct: **8:33 a.m., 7 o'clock**
    Incorrect: **Route/490 east**   Correct: **Route 490/east**

6. Never divide a number.

    Incorrect: **(761)/061-7238**   Correct: **(761) 061-7238**
    Incorrect: **Account No. 131-/4156**   Correct: **Account No. 131-4156**

7. Never divide a two-part proper noun.

    Incorrect: **Ms. Mary/Lee Marco**   Correct: **Ms. Mary Lee/Marco**
    Incorrect: **Los/Angeles airport**   Correct: **Los Angeles/airport**

8. Only divide a street address before the words *Street, Road*, etc.

    Incorrect: **176/Fifth Avenue**   Correct: **176 Fifth/Avenue**
    Incorrect: **15/West 32 Street**   Correct: **15 West 32/Street**

9. Divide a hyphenated word only at its own hyphen; do not add any hyphens.

    Incorrect: **daugh/ter-in-law**   Correct: **daughter-in-/law**
    Incorrect: **well-mean/ing**   Correct: **well-/meaning**

■ **Tips for Word Processors**

When working on a computer, you enter a "CODED," "HARD," or "REQUIRED" space between items that must remain together on the same line. Please refer to your specific software's instruction manual.

Word Division Rules

You divide words at the end of lines to keep the lines approximately equal in length. In word processing, word division is called hyphenation, and it reduces the amount of extra spaces between words in justified lines of type. Once their hyphenation program is activated, some word processing programs will offer correct word division options. If yours does not, use a dictionary and follow these rules.

RULE	EXAMPLE
1. Divide a word only between syllables.	friend-ship
2. Divide compound words between the root words.	sun-light
3. Divide hyphenated words only at the point of the hyphen.	father-in-law
4. Leave at least 2 letters of a word on the first line and carry at least 3 letters to the next line.	en-tered truck-ers
5. Divide words after a prefix.	pre-scribe
6. Divide a word before a suffix.	predica-ment
7. When a word ends in "tion", divide before it.	perfec-tion
8. When 2 consonants are preceded and followed by vowels, divide the word BETWEEN the consonants.	al-bums
9. Divide words between doubled consonants.	mil-lion
10. When a suffix causes the final consonant to double, divide the double letters.	stop-ping begin-ning
11. If the word ended in double letters before the suffix was added, divide before the suffix.	press-ing
12. When a word ends with a consonant followed by *le*, those 3 letters form the last syllable.	spin-dle
13. Words containing a single vowel syllable should be divided after that syllable UNLESS the ending syllables are *bly, ble, cle,* or *cal*.	sepa-rate rad-ical

Rule	Example
14. When 2 one-letter syllables occur together within a word, divide between them.	gradu-ation
15. Sometimes words are divided differently depending on their part of speech.	rec-ord (noun) re-cord (verb)

NEVER DIVIDE

Rule	Example
1. One-syllable words	shopped
2. Words of 5 or fewer letters	enter
3. Acronyms	ILGWU
4. Contractions	shouldn't
5. Numbers	067-04-7518
6. Proper nouns (names, dates, or places)	September Mr. Andropolus Minneapolis
7. The last word on a page	

■ **Tips for Word Processors**

Follow the rules listed above when using the hyphenation feature. To divide words, turn hyphenation on and then confirm the location of the hyphen in each word the computer highlights (usually by manually positioning the cursor). Most software will NOT break words only in the correct location. Remember, a computer cannot recognize a proper name, determine if a word has more than one syllable, or realize that a hyphenated number should not be separated. Please refer to your software's instruction manual for specific hyphenation feature directions.

Frequently Confused or Misused Words

Accept/Except

Accept (to receive): `Please accept my apology for the delay.`
Except (to exclude, but): `Everyone was there except Jason.`

Affect/Effect

Affect (to influence): `The bad news didn't affect her at all!`
Effect (use when you can substitute *result*): `What effect will this mark have on my course average?`
Effect (to bring about): `How do you plan to effect this change in policy?`

All ready/Already

All ready (use when you can substitute *prepared*): `We were all ready for the camping trip.`
Already (before this time): `We had already packed for the trip.`

All together/Altogether

All together (as a group): `Let's sing it all together.`
Altogether (use when you can substitute *entirely*): `This is an altogether different issue.`

Among/Between

Among (refers to 3 or more persons/things): `I moved among the class members.`
Between (refers to 2 persons/things): `Between you and me, I think it's the truth.`

Amount/Number

Amount (groups of items that CANNOT be counted; singular nouns): `What amount of damage was sustained as a result of the hurricane?`
Number (items that CAN be counted; plural nouns): `A number of lawyers protested the ruling.`

Any one/Anyone

Any one (ALWAYS followed by *of*): `Please hand me any one of those books.`
Anyone (any person): `Anyone can operate this software package.`

Any time/Anytime

Any time (an unspecified time): `You may respond any time before June 30.`
Anytime (at any time whatever; use when able to substitute *whenever*): `Be sure to call us anytime you have a question.`

Bad/Badly

Bad (used with the verbs *feel* and *look*): **I feel bad about Mark's injury.**
Badly (used with all other verbs): **I did badly on the test.**

Biannual/Biennial

Biannual (happening twice annually): **You will be issued biannual checks.**
Biennial (happening every second year): **Since their terms are two years, the council's election is a biennial event.**

Capitol/Capital

Capitol (building in which a legislature meets): **The rally was held outside the state capitol.**
Capital (use for all other meanings): **The capital of Wisconsin is Madison.**

Complement/Compliment

Complement (to complete or perfect): **Those curtains will complement the wallpaper in that room.**
Compliment (to praise): **She accepted his compliment graciously.**

Conscience/Conscious

Conscience (ability to know right from wrong): **Her guilty conscience eventually made her confess to the crime.**
Conscious (mentally aware): **It was not a conscious decision on my part.**

Desert/Dessert

Desert (hot, dry land): **The desert stretched for miles.**
Dessert (tasty treat after a meal): **Which dessert has fewer calories?**

Emigrate/Immigrate

Emigrate (to move FROM a country): **We decided to emigrate from Poland to the USA.**
Immigrate (to move TO a country): **How many Mexicans immigrate to the USA annually?**

Every day/Everyday

Every day (use when you can substitute *each day*): **Every day I walk to the corner to buy the newspaper.**
Everyday (ordinary): **It was an everyday type of occurrence.**

Every one/Everyone

Every one (ALWAYS followed by *of*): **Every one of our cars is guaranteed.**
Everyone (all the people in a group): **Have you met everyone here?**

Farther/Further

Farther (use for distance): **It is farther to Waco than to Dallas.**
Further (additional): **For further details, please call me.**

Its/It's

Its (possessive form of it): **The dog bit its own tail.**
It's (use when you can substitute *it is, it has,* or *it was*): **It's a shame that you cannot join us for the party.**

Lay/Lie

Lay (use when you can substitute *place*): **Please do not lay the book on that table.**
Lie (to recline): **The doctor recommends that I lie down each day.**

Passed/Past

Passed (to go by; circulate): **She passed the car at 65 miles per hour.**
Past (time gone by): **In the past we did honor those requests.**

Precede/Proceed

Precede (to go before): **You should precede me in the procession.**
Proceed (to continue): **Please proceed with your discussion.**

Principle/Principal

Principle (rule; belief): **Many people live by the principle of do unto others as you would have them do unto you.**
Principal (use for all other meanings): **That's the principal reason for this special meeting.**

Raise/Rise

Raise (to increase; to physically lift): **She raised $45,000 for the cause.**
Rise (to get up without assistance): **The bread will rise overnight.**

Some time/Sometime

Some time (a period of time): **It was some time before the baby slept through the night.**
Sometime (at an indefinite time): **Give me a call sometime.**

Stationary/Stationery

Stationary (fixed in position): **I exercised on a stationary bike.**
Stationery (writing materials): **Ada needs to reorder the stationery supplies.**

Their/There/They're

Their (possessive of *they*): **Their child is the valedictorian.**
There (at that point): **There was a great deal of confusion.**
They're (use when you can substitute *they are*): **They're in charge while Roberto is gone.**

To/Too/Two

To (a preposition): **I have to see it to believe it.**
Too (also; excessive): **It was too hot in the theater.**
Two (a number): **Only two people attended the open house.**

Was/Were

Was (past tense of verb *to be*): **He was happy with the results.**
Were (ALWAYS used after *if, as if, as though,* or *wish*): **If I were Ms. Dalton, I would invest in the stock market.**

Who/Whom

Who (use as a subject or when you can substitute *he*): **We disagreed over who should be the first speaker.**
Whom (use as an object or when you can substitute *him*): **Whom would you choose to represent our interests?**

Whose/Who's

Whose (possessive of *who*): **Whose jacket is this?**
Who's (use when you can substitute *who is* or *who has*): **Who's going to the fair on Friday?**

Your/You're

Your (possessive of *you*): **Your house is beautiful!**
You're (use when you can substitute *you are*): **You're a dedicated profes-sional.**

Capitalization Rules

You should capitalize in the following situations:

1. The first word in a sentence or a quotation:

    Your copy of the purchase offer is enclosed.
    Laura said, "Let's turn left at this intersection."

2. Proper nouns--the names of SPECIFIC people, places, and things:

    Mr. Frederick Chomsky
    Albion, New York
    Tupperware bowls (the specific brand name is capitalized)
    <u>The New York Times</u>

3. The first word in the salutation and complimentary closing of a letter:

    Dear Mrs. Eckert:
    Sincerely yours,

4. The days of the week, months of the year, and holidays. Seasons are NOT capitalized:

    Monday
    May 27
    Memorial Day
    summer

5. A person's title only when it comes before the name:

    Vice President Lyell Cantwell
    Lyell Cantwell, vice president of marketing

6. SPECIFIC organizational departments only WITHIN your own company:

    the Research Division
    their research division

7. SPECIFIC parts of the country:

    She lives in the Midwest.
    It's located about five miles east of town.